**Endorsements fo**

"This is a beautiful, clear, and well-written book. Thanks to Nathan Tidridge for producing a great piece of scholarship, research, and good feeling. I definitely recommend this book."
— Professor John Borrows, Canada Research Chair in Indigenous Law

"It is my privilege as a lieutenant governor of Ontario who was deeply involved in Aboriginal matters during my term to strongly recommend Nathan Tidridge's latest book, *The Queen at the Council Fire*. It is a must-read for anyone wanting to understand the history of the relationship between the Crown and Indigenous peoples and why that relationship is crucial to Canada's future relations with First Nations."
— Honourable David C. Onley, O.Ont., 28th Lieutenant Governor of Ontario

"With *The Queen at the Council Fire*, Nathan Tidridge has gifted us a concise, sharp, and detailed account of one of the most important events in Canada's history, a moment all too often ignored in the history books."
— Niigaanwewidam James Sinclair, Associate Professor, Department of Native Studies, University of Manitoba

"Constitutional monarchy is usually discussed in terms of *principles*. This account demonstrates that when the subject is First Nations, it is the *practices* of the Crown in its long relationship with Indigenous peoples that are of paramount concern. Through the prism of the Crown, Nathan Tidridge offers a unique perspective on a subject of fundamental importance."
— Dr. David Smith, Author of *The Invisible Crown: The First Principle of Canadian Government*

"Nathan Tidridge has given us a richly textured account of the historic meeting of First Nations with Sir William Johnson, the British Monarch's personal representative, at Niagara in 1764. The Treaty of Niagara is Canada's first Confederation. Tidridge's book is must reading for understanding Canada's constitutional foundations."
— Dr. Peter Russell, Professor Emeritus of Political Science at the University of Toronto

"The Covenant Chain is a metaphor for alliance between the Crown and various Indigenous nations. This metaphor is represented on wampum belts by two men holding hands or two men holding a chain, bound together by the silver chain of friendship. In old councils, both participants of the treaty had to re-tell the 'talk' on the belt to demonstrate their understanding of the mutual obligations. Long ago, the representatives of the Crown had let go their end of the belt and had quit coming to the council fire to 'polish the chain.' In this book, Mr. Tidridge offers a re-telling of the 'talk' from a modern-day Canadian perspective."
— Alan Corbiere, Anishinaabe Cultural Historian,
M'Chigeeng First Nation

"In *The Queen at the Council Fire*, Nathan Tidridge demonstrates the link between Canadian federalism and the First Nations, debunking the assumption that 'Indians' are simply an issue for Ottawa. Mr. Tidridge encourages us to look beyond the stereotypes and appreciate the mutual interest of both orders of government in collaborating with the First Nations through the unique institution of the Canadian Crown."
— D. Michael Jackson, CVO, SOM, CD, Author of *The Crown and Canadian Federalism* (Dundurn, 2013),
Vice-President, Institute for the Study of the Crown in Canada

"Nathan Tidridge offers a thoughtful and rich interpretation of the Treaty of Niagara, highlighting the Covenant Chain and its direct relationship with Indigenous peoples. The Queen at the Council Fire is an important read for educators and the greater community to help facilitate respectful and meaningful conversations about mutual obligations, relationship building, and aspects of reconciliation."
— Dr. Jenny Kay Dupuis, Member of the Nipissing First Nation

"Nathan draws the reader into an important story about a little known and often complex subject. Nya:weh Nathan for all of your hard work, passion, and friendship."
— Heather George, Acting Cultural Coordinator of Her Majesty's Royal Chapel of the Mohawks, Cultural Coordinator of Chiefswood National Historic Site

# THE QUEEN AT THE COUNCIL FIRE

### The Treaty of Niagara, Reconciliation, and the Dignified Crown in Canada

## NATHAN TIDRIDGE

The Institute for the Study of the Crown in Canada (ISCC)
at Massey College

**DUNDURN**
TORONTO

Copyright © Nathan Tidridge, 2015

All rights reserved. No part of this publication may be reproduced, stored in a retrieval system, or transmitted in any form or by any means, electronic, mechanical, photocopying, recording, or otherwise (except for brief passages for purpose of review) without the prior permission of Dundurn Press. Permission to photocopy should be requested from Access Copyright.

Editor: Dominic Farrell
Design: Janette Thompson (Jansom)
Cover design: Courtney Horner
Cover image: The Honourable Ralph Steinhauer reads the Speech from the Throne in his full Native regalia on January 23, 1975. *Courtesy of Provincial Archives of Alberta, 33167/3.*
Printer: Webcom

**Library and Archives Canada Cataloguing in Publication**

Tidridge, Nathan, 1978-, author
        The queen at the council fire : the Treaty of Niagara, reconciliation, and the dignified Crown in Canada / Nathan Tidridge.

(The Crown in Canada)
Includes bibliographical references and index.
Issued in print and electronic formats.
ISBN 978-1-4597-3066-3 (bound).--ISBN 978-1-4597-3067-0 (pdf).--ISBN 978-1-4597-3068-7 (epub)

        1. Treaty of Niagara (1764). 2. Indians of North America--Canada--Treaties. 3. Indians of North America--Canada--Government relations. 4. Indians of North America--Legal status, laws, etc.--Canada. 5. Monarchy--Canada--History. 6. Canada--History--To 1763 (New France). 7. Canada--History--1763-1867. I. Title. II. Series: Crown in Canada (Series)

KE7709.T53 2015         342.7108'72         C2015-900565-5
                                            C2015-900566-3
KF8205 T53 2015

1  2  3  4  5    19  18  17  16  15

We acknowledge the support of the **Canada Council for the Arts** and the **Ontario Arts Council** for our publishing program. We also acknowledge the financial support of the **Government of Canada** through the **Canada Book Fund** and **Livres Canada Books**, and the **Government of Ontario** through the **Ontario Book Publishing Tax Credit** and the **Ontario Media Development Corporation**.

Care has been taken to trace the ownership of copyright material used in this book. The author and the publisher welcome any information enabling them to rectify any references or credits in subsequent editions.

— *J. Kirk Howard, President*

The publisher is not responsible for websites or their content unless they are owned by the publisher.

Printed and bound in Canada.

VISIT US AT
Dundurn.com | @dundurnpress | Facebook.com/dundurnpress | Pinterest.com/dundurnpress

Dundurn
3 Church Street, Suite 500
Toronto, Ontario, Canada
M5E 1M2

All profits generated from this book will be donated to
The Lieutenant Governor's Aboriginal Summer Reading Camps managed by
Frontier College on behalf of the Office of the Lieutenant Governor of Ontario.

Dedicated to my wife, Christine Vanderwal.
A passionate educator, Christine is actively engaged
in fostering reconciliation, helping the Canada
she loves reach its full potential. I explore
these waters together with her.

# Table of Contents

| | | |
|---|---|---|
| | Acknowledgements | 9 |
| | Introduction | 11 |
| CHAPTER ONE | Encountering Indigenous Voices | 29 |
| CHAPTER TWO | The 1764 Treaty of Niagara and Covenant Chain of Friendship | 49 |
| CHAPTER THREE | The Queen at the Council Fire | 77 |
| CHAPTER FOUR | Building Community — A Model Royal Visit | 119 |
| CHAPTER FIVE | Suggestions for Moving Forward Together | 129 |
| | Notes | 155 |
| | Bibliography | 169 |
| | Index | 175 |
| | About the Author | 182 |

# Acknowledgements

This book began as an essay written to highlight the importance of the Treaty of Niagara and its relationship to the offices of the Canadian Crown. This journey has brought me into contact with many people, including great teachers, knowledge keepers, elders, and good friends. All of them have helped develop my respect of the Covenant Chain and the treaty that extended it into these lands.

Here I acknowledge and thank Dr. John Borrows (Canada Research Chair in Indigenous Law at the University of Victoria Law School), Mr. Nick Bridges (University of Ottawa), Mr. Alan Corbiere (Anishinaabe Cultural Historian, M'Chigeeng First Nation), Mr. Richard Berthelsen (Managing Director, Institute for the Study of the Crown in Canada at Massey College), Dr. Jenny Dupuis (Member of the Nipissing First Nation), Mr. Dominic Farrell (my extraordinary editor with Dundurn Press), Ms. Heather George (Cultural Coordinator, Chiefswood National Historic Site and Her Majesty's Royal Chapel of the Mohawks), Ms. Jane Gibson (Natural History/Natural Heritage Inc.), Mr. James Hammond (Private Secretary) and the Office of the Lieutenant Governor of British Columbia, Mr. Rick Hill (The Six Nations Legacy Consortium), Mr. Kirk Howard (Founder and President of Dundurn Press), Mr. Anthony Hylton (Private Secretary) and the Office of the Lieutenant Governor of

Ontario (particularly Mr. Eugene Berezovsky and Mr. John Gross), Mr. Sean Kearney (McMaster University), Ms. Carolyn King (Mississaugas of the New Credit First Nation), Dr. Philippe Lagassé (Associate Professor of Public and International Affairs, University of Ottawa), Mr. Ken Maracle (Faith Keeper of the Lower Cayuga Longhouse, Member of the Cayuga Nation), Dr. Christopher McCreery (Private Secretary) and the Office of the Lieutenant Governor of Nova Scotia, the Honourable David C. Onley (Twenty-Eighth Lieutenant Governor of Ontario), Mrs. Ruth Ann Onley, Mr. Barry Penhale (Publisher Emeritus, Dundurn Press), the Honourable Steven L. Point (Twenty-Eighth Lieutenant Governor of British Columbia), Cheryl Red Eagle and the Staff at the Woodland Cultural Centre, Dr. Peter Russell (Professor Emeritus of Political Science at the University of Toronto), Ms. Heather Salloum (Private Secretary and Executive Director) and the Office of the Lieutenant Governor of Saskatchewan, Elder Garry Sault (Mississaugas of the New Credit First Nation), Dr. David Smith (Distinguished Visiting Professor in the Department of Politics and Public Administration and a Member of the Yeates School of Graduate Studies at Ryerson University), Professor Thomas H.B. Symons (Vanier Professor Emeritus and Founding President of Trent University), and Ms. Barb Walline (Private Secretary) and the Office of the Lieutenant Governor of Alberta.

I am honoured that *The Queen at the Council Fire* launches **The Institute for the Study of the Crown in Canada (ISCC) at Massey College**, a series of books being developed through a partnership between Dundurn Press and the Institute for the Study of the Crown in Canada at Massey College. This collection recognizes the tremendous contributions made by Kirk Howard in educating Canadians about their constitutional monarchy. Kirk is a remarkable man, and his decades of work in preserving Canadian history, identity, and culture will have lasting effects for generations to come.

# Introduction

I do not have Indigenous ancestry.

In writing a book like this I must declare that I do not own any of the Indigenous stories and perspectives that circle the Treaty of Niagara, the Covenant Chain, or any of the experiences surrounding such places as residential schools. Rather, I look at these stories from the outside, as a Canadian who wants to respect and honour First Nations by trying to understand the nature of the relationships between Indigenous and

"Indian Chief's Medal" presented by the Crown to commemorate Treaties Three, Four, Five, Six, Seven, and Eight. Queen Victoria's effigy is depicted on the obverse of the medal. *Library and Archives Canada, Acc. No. 1964-1-1-M.*

non-Indigenous peoples in Canada — relationships that have been broken for a long time.

There are over 650 distinct First Nations, as well as Métis and Inuit peoples, in this part of North America (known as Turtle Island in many Indigenous cultures), each with their own stories. All of these are important to our collective understanding of the land we share. A clear vision can only be achieved if everyone's stories are heard and respected, although such a thing can never be fully accomplished. For the past two years I have been exploring the Covenant Chain, the symbol of the relationship created between the Haudenosaunee and the Dutch in 1613, established with the Wabanaki Confederacy in 1725, extended to the Anishinaabe in 1764, and gradually applied to many First Nations across the continent. With the withdrawal of the Dutch from North America, this relationship was transferred to the French Crown and then the British Crown. In Canada, it now resides with the Canadian Crown, the heir of the rights and responsibilities of the British Crown in Canada.

While encountering the communities that have marked this journey, I have learned that some things in history are never meant to fully crystallize.

Most writers on the subject of Indigenous peoples and their relationships with Canada, however, have seen no such difficulty in trying to pin things down. In reading on the subject myself, I have encountered an astonishing variety of labels and identifiers. Through all of this, however, I have kept in mind the words of a young philosopher, Tyler Alexis, who attended one of my classes. He wrote in his journal, "labels remove identity." These words are now framed and displayed in my classroom.

The primacy of the word *Indian* as a label for the largest group of Indigenous peoples in Canada was cemented by its use in the infamous 1876 Indian Act, and the word remains the legal term for a member of this group today, bestowed, depending on the blood quantum of the individual no less, by the Government of Canada. (The government further labels this group of Indigenous peoples by subdividing them into

# INTRODUCTION

Status and non-Status Indians). There are, of course, other groups of Indigenous peoples in Canada. They are recognized by the Canadian Constitution, which labels them as Métis and Inuit.

While the word *Indian* is often used by many people (Indigenous and non-Indigenous alike), I choose to not use it within these pages. As someone outside of the Indigenous community, I feel that the word is too loaded down with history for me to use it — in saying this, however, I also have to emphasize that I have no right to reject the term's use by people who have been raised knowing no other name for themselves.

Other names for the Indigenous peoples of Canada have emerged in the past few decades: Aboriginal peoples (a term also created by the Canadian government), Indigenous peoples, and First Nations. Finding the right term is hard, especially in these evolving times when Canadians are rediscovering relationships that are meant to be both active and collaborative.

My rule of thumb for this book has been to try, whenever possible, to use the actual name of each Nation (if it is hard to pronounce, it becomes incumbent upon us to learn how to read it as part of the journey toward reconciliation). When speaking in general terms, I have elected to use the identifiers *Aboriginal* and *Indigenous peoples*, as well as *First Nations*. While I may be using terms created by the Canadian government, and widely adopted by Indigenous peoples, this book rejects the parameters imposed on these terms by the Indian Act. Put simply, while I may use the term *Aboriginal*, I reject the definition for this word created by the federal Ministry of Aboriginal Affairs and Northern Development (and thus the Indian Act); instead, I use it as a general term to encompass the many peoples whose ancestors were once the lone stewards of the lands now called Canada.

The term *First Nation* automatically raises the issue of sovereignty, since political discourse tends to equate nationhood with sovereignty. This book does not try to define the relationship between nationhood and sovereignty or what sovereignty legally means in this country.

The term gets thrown around a lot when discussing First Nations and Canada — I have been as guilty of doing this as others. With interactions between Indigenous peoples and Canada articulated as being "Nation to Nation" relationships, a concrete definition of what sovereignty actually means in such a context needs to be developed and ratified by all treaty parties. (Does Indigenous nationhood equate to sovereignty within Canada? Or, does it require a separate political unit that would exist in association with the Canadian state?)

While deciding all of this may be a nearly impossible task, it must be admitted that the status quo no longer works. What has been made very clear to me over the past two years I've spent researching this topic is that if First Nations and Canada are to make any meaningful progress, our relationships — and the terms used to describe them — must be clearly renewed and/or redefined.

Peter Russell discussed the problems involved in defining (and redefining) sovereignty in the context of Canada/First Nation relationships in an essay exploring the 2014 awarding of common law title over their land to the Tsilhqot'in Nation by the Supreme Court of Canada.[1] Remarking that the ruling of the Supreme Court of Canada to reverse the British Columbia Court's decision to deny Indigenous title was a victory for Indigenous peoples, Russell writes:

> … it also marks the limits to which their relationship with the settler society will be decolonized. The Supreme Court of Canada … is an institution of the settler society.… The members of this court accept the imposition of British sovereignty and of its successor state, Canada, over Indigenous Nations. Aboriginal title is considered to be a "burden" on the Crown's radical (i.e., underlying) title to all the territory over which it declares sovereignty.

Russell goes on to quote American chief justice John Marshall, who acknowledged in 1823 that the "imposition of foreign rule on free peoples while pragmatically necessary was contrary to the principles of natural law."[2]

Treaties are relationships — living relationships. Grounded in love, relationships can be beautiful, intense, raucous affairs. Remember that loving someone does not always mean that you will necessarily like them all of the time. In one moment you and your partner can be completely on the same page; in the next you are isolated from each other. Sadly, love can so often turn to hate, passion to loathing.

Just as relationships change, so, too, do the participants in any relationship. In Canada, the Crown is a dynamic and fluid institution, and has evolved to meet the needs of a complex federation while at the same time being bound to First Nations across the land. Far from being a colonial artifact, Canada's living and evolving constitutional monarchy is as integral to the Constitution of this country as bones are to our bodies.

Interest in the nature and role of the Canadian Crown is certainly widespread in the legal and academic communities in this country. However, interest in the subject goes beyond that. Among the exciting developments to come out of the regular academic meetings held around the study of the Canadian Crown since the historic June 10, 2010, Ottawa conference, *The Crown in Canada: Present Realities and Future Options*, co-chaired by Senators Serge Joyal and Hugh Segal, are the substantial conversations around the relationship between the Canadian Crown and First Nations. These conversations have proven of abiding interest to First Nations communities. Indeed, a subsequent conference on the subject, the 2012 Regina conference, *The Crown in Canada: A Diamond Jubilee Assessment*, was co-sponsored by the Whitecap Dakota First Nation (western allies of the British Crown during the War of 1812). The publications that have flowed from these conferences testify to the renewed interest in the study of this institution by First Nations and those interested in rekindling the knowledge around the Crown/First Nations relationship.

The King's Fire being lit at sunrise near the site of Niagara-on-the-Lake's Indian Council House on August 2, 2014. *Courtesy of author.*

I was privileged to attend the commemorations of the 250th anniversary of the Treaty of Niagara held by the Association of Iroquois and Allied Indians, the Chiefs of Ontario, and the Six Nations Legacy Consortium from August 1 to 2, 2014, at Fort Niagara and the site of the Indian Council House on The Commons of Niagara-on-the-Lake. During those two days I saw the wampum displayed in the "French Castle" of Fort Niagara, smoked the Unity Pipe given to Grand Council Chief Pat Madahbee, witnessed the Ontario government (represented by the Honourable David Zimmer, minister of aboriginal affairs) present two strings of wampum to each of the original twenty-four nations that gathered for the 1764 Niagara Council, and saw the effects of Lieutenant-Governor David C. Onley's displays of respect on the assembled delegates (His Honour, wearing his medal as an Honorary Witness of the Truth and Reconciliation Commission, attended the August 1 event at Fort Niagara).

## INTRODUCTION

From the beginning of my research, I decided that, as I read more information and encountered new people, I would write an essay on the subject that would be allowed to grow and evolve as I learned more (a growth that extended far beyond the draft that was sent to the offices of the governor general and the lieutenant governor of Ontario in the winter of 2014). *The Queen at the Council Fire* is the result.

Rather than offer any answers (the one-way conversations that books create make such an offering problematic), I hope that this book acts as a starting point for others to understand that we once sat together with First Nations in a true (and often tumultuous) relationship. In all of this, the Dignified Crown acted as an effective conduit to demonstrate respect and facilitate communication — a role it is rekindling across Canada today.

I use the term *Dignified Crown* deliberately, invoking English political writer Walter Bagehot's distinction between the dignified (largely ceremonial) and efficient (powers now exercised by elected ministers) aspects of the Crown outlined in his seminal work *The English Constitution*. For a concrete definition I go to the cornerstone of any serious study of the Canadian Crown, Dr. David Smith's *The Invisible Crown: The First Principle of Canadian Government*. Smith explains Bagehot's role of the Dignified Crown (or Monarch) as follows:

> … the Monarch (or Crown, since Bagehot used both terms) has been viewed as a dignified element whose duties are essentially passive: personifying (the State), symbolizing (morality), and representing (society). Passive but not unimportant, since if performed well, the dignified Crown, according to Bagehot, evoked loyalty and confirmed political order.[3]

Dr. Smith goes on to caution, however, that the Canadian experience of constitutional monarchy demands a level of participation by the vice-regal representatives (the governors general and lieutenant governors) that would be unthinkable by its British counterpart. The frequency of minority governments in Canada and its provinces has thrust the Queen's representatives into the political and public spotlights. Recent events such as the 2008 prorogation of Parliament have demonstrated how Canada's incarnation of constitutional monarchy occasionally places the Dignified Crown on the political stage. First Nations, however, see it as having a more permanent role in our Canadian theatre.

The Dignified Crown has a unique role in Canada — one that has been largely ignored over the past centuries. Added to the roles of personifying, symbolizing, and representing the Queen as the State, the Dignified Crown in this country has the duty, according to First Nations, to maintain ancient relationships with them that are deeply personal. I have learned that the relationships between the Monarch and First Nations are integral to honouring the treaties and reconciling their sad legacy with Canada. Often in Canada the Queen is an abstraction, her name evoked with the understanding that Elizabeth II herself has nothing to do with the day-to-day operation of the state. Using Smith's interpretation of Bagehot, Her Majesty is a passive element in our constitutional workings. Not so for First Nations.

The Monarch detailed in the treaties is an active one, a figure in direct relationship with the Indigenous population who has a duty to ensure that the Canadian government lives up to its obligations. The Indigenous and non-Indigenous expectations of the Dignified Crown — evolving separately since the moment of First Contact — have left the Queen and (especially) her Canadian representatives grasping to meet the needs of peoples that have radically different perspectives of their offices. This book explores these contradicting experiences and offers some concrete ways in which the Dignified Crown can further the cause of reconciliation of Indigenous and non-Indigenous peoples in meaningful and active ways that respect both perspectives.

During the final stages of writing *The Queen at the Council Fire*, the Countess of Wessex initiated a visit to the northern Ontario community of Kitchenuhmaykoosib Inninuwug (KI), inviting a distinguished party of women that included the premier of Ontario, the spouses of both the lieutenant governor and the American ambassador, as well as the lieutenant governor–designate of the province. During this remarkable Royal tour, the countess actively demonstrated one of the most important and relevant roles held by the Dignified Crown of Canada in the twenty-first century: the ability to build community in the name of reconciliation. Explored more in Chapter Four, the work of the Earl and Countess of Wessex has done much to polish the Silver Covenant Chain of Friendship.

An important part of my journey to understand Indigenous history included the recreation of the 1764 Covenant Chain Wampum presented by Sir William Johnson to the Western Nations of the Great Lakes watershed assembled at Niagara. Thanks to the support of publisher Kirk Howard and Dundurn Press, as well as a generous grant from the Ontario Arts Council, I was able to commission Ken Maracle to recreate the wampum during the winter of 2014. Maracle completed the belt in the presence of my wife, Christine Vanderwal, some of my students and their parents,[4] and me at his home in the territory of the Six Nations of the Grand River. This location recalls that the ancient chain the wampum is meant to represent had originally been established between the Haudenosaunee and the Crown before extending north into Anishinaabe lands.[5]

For the nearly two hours that it took Ken to weave the final rows of glass beads into the sinew and threads of the wampum (concluding over forty hours of work),[6] we talked about its symbolism, as well as anything else that happened to come up during our time together (weather, children, our work).

Wampum takes a long time to create.

"That's the point," Ken explained to us. "It means that it is important." The time Maracle spent creating the wampum, the intimacy and

Christine Vanderwal watches while Ken Maracle completes the 1764 Covenant Chain Wampum replica at his home on the Territory of the Six Nations of the Grand River. March 8, 2014. *Courtesy of author.*

INTRODUCTION

focus it gave him, the stories it conjured for the people around him as he worked, imbued it with energy.

While a replica, Ken explained that the wampum had power — that the stories manifested in it remain and are living. Countless students and others will bear witness to this belt and the Treaty it preserves.

The 1764 Covenant Chain Wampum is a Canadian artifact — it was originally created by the British Crown to perpetuate a living familial relationship that they had helped create. In fact, many of the images on the wampum (the date and the way the figures are rendered) would not have been used by Indigenous peoples. The creation of this replica is not an instance of a non-Indigenous person trying to interpret and claim an

Ken Maracle's Covenant Chain Wampum replica is displayed during the Honouring Voices Symposium hosted by Waterdown District High School May 6, 2014. The replica is displayed with other wampum created by Yvonne Thomas of the Jake Thomas Learning Centre. Suspended overhead is University of Windsor artist Alex MacKay's *Treaty Canoe*.[7] *Courtesy of author.*

Indigenous artifact; rather, it is an example of a Canadian rediscovering his ancestors' shared vision for the country.

Ken's replica has been at the centre of my classroom in Waterdown District High School ever since, creating conversation and triggering explorations of a relationship that was intended to be kept strong. As a teaching tool, the replica wampum has been invaluable, but as Ken said to me as he placed it in my hands, there is an energy that lives within the beads and sinew.

During her retirement speech, a colleague of mine, Cindy Everest, explained that teaching is like throwing a stone into a pool of water — ripples radiate out from an educator and spread into the world. These ripples encounter others, creating new waves that bounce off and embrace new individuals and their ideas — a vision of the Earth engulfed in these waves immediately came to my mind after Cindy spoke that day. It is this image that I now see when I think of Ken's wampum.

A few years ago, yet another housing subdivision broke ground in my hometown of Waterdown, Ontario. Residential development in the green fields surrounding Waterdown, a suburb of Hamilton, was nothing new. Before the flattening of the rolling hills of the Waterdown South Development, an archeological study was done in 2005 revealing 105 "sites of interest." All but one of these sites contained Indigenous artifacts — some in significant quantities. Ultimately, a handful of these sites were excavated before houses started going up and the remaining land was paved. The many arrowheads, axe heads, and pieces from lives lived many centuries ago now sit in someone's garage (they are owned by the private archeological company contracted to do the excavations).

Not all of the land of "Waterdown South" was disturbed, and a twenty-seven-acre tract surrounding Grindstone Creek was spared the bulldozers along with the twenty or so Indigenous sites within its bounds. In the spirit of the Treaty of Niagara, a committee of local citizens (including teachers and students) was formed with myself

INTRODUCTION

as chair.[8] Our goal was a simple one: To educate the community that the Waterdown-Flamborough Region had been home to Indigenous peoples for thousands of years, and the Waterdown South Development specifically had 104 Aboriginal sites located within it.[9]

An important part of this project involved consulting with the traditional owners of the land Waterdown was located on. Elder Garry Sault of the Mississaugas of the New Credit guided the committee through the Indigenous history of Waterdown and Flamborough, and stood with us as we formally asked Chief M. Bryan Laforme and the Council of the Mississaugas of the New Credit First Nation for their endorsement and support of the initiative. In writing to the council, the Treaty of Niagara was invoked along with the hope that the Souharissen Natural Area (named by Ishkwegiizhig — Eugene Kahgee — of the Saugeen First Nation No. 29) would in some way polish the Silver Covenant Chain.

The dedication ceremony was held on August 21, 2014, and attended by members of the Indigenous and non-Indigenous communities. The Souharrisen Natural Area was jointly dedicated by the Honourable David C. Onley, lieutenant governor of Ontario, and Chief M. Bryan Laforme. Before the event, the first Sacred Fire in generations (perhaps centuries) was lit in Flamborough and later visited by the lieutenant governor, the chief, the local member of Parliament (David Sweet), and members of the community.

"The Treaty of Niagara Covenant Wampum Belt provided the inspiration for this moment," remarked Chief Laforme during the dedication, "May today mark the renewal of those pledges of peace and friendship made over two hundred years ago.… May this mark the beginning of a new partnership between the people of this region and our First Nation."[10]

One of my favourite moments was when Carolyn King,[11] Hamilton councillor Judi Partridge, Chief Laforme, and Lieutenant Governor Onley painted a stencil of a Mississauga moccasin on the sidewalk

The Honourable David C. Onley and Chief M. Bryan Laforme dedicate the twenty-seven-acre Souharissen Natural Area in Waterdown, Ontario, on August 21, 2014. *Courtesy of Christopher Rivait.*

facing the monument stone. Carolyn explained to the gathered crowd that the moccasin marked her traditional territory, and it now fell to local students to return in future years to touch up the paint (metaphorically polishing the Covenant Chain). Students have been visiting the site ever since.

Following the formal dedication, a reception was held at my home, where members of the community were joined by the Queen's representative and chief of the Mississauagas for a feast to celebrate the First Nations' formal return to their traditional territory after an absence of over two hundred years. Called "The Reception by the Pond," the gathering was held in our back garden, where Ken Maracle's replica Covenant Chain Wampum was proudly displayed. Waterdown and Flamborough's Indigenous identity was rekindled and affirmed that day in the spirit of the Treaty of Niagara, and the Souharissen Natural Area continues to create community and build new relationships.

INTRODUCTION

The Souharissen Monument Stone unveiled August 21, 2014. *Courtesy of author.*

• 25 •

Stencil of a Mississauga moccasin on the sidewalk facing the Souharissen Monument Stone in Waterdown, Ontario. *Courtesy of author.*

This book explores a path toward reconciliation. I now recognize that such a journey may never fully be realized, but I have learned that's not necessarily the point. I recognize that *The Queen at the Council Fire* is rooted in my personal journey, but have learned that there is no other way it could be.

Truly this has been a journey of lessons, and to quote photojournalist Dan Eldon, "The journey is the destination." In writing this book, I hope in some small way I am helping make the chain bright again.

Nathan Tidridge
Waterdown, Ontario
On the traditional territory of the Chonnonton and Mississaugas of the New Credit Nations.**

---

**A portion of this book was composed on the traditional territory of the Mi'kmaq of Epekwitk (Prince Edward Island).

INTRODUCTION

The first Sacred Fire lit in Flamborough, Ontario, in generations. The fire was started by Elder Garry Sault of the Mississaugas of the New Credit First Nation, and Rocky Burnham of the Six Nations of the Grand River acted as fire keeper. *Courtesy of author.*

CHAPTER ONE

# Encountering Indigenous Voices

My first encounter with Indigenous history stemmed from my boyhood explorations of the lake at my family cottage in Muskoka. Buck Lake, pooling out from either side of the Muskoka-Parry Sound border, was the source of many adventures as I plied its waters in an old canoe.[1] I had burned all the official maps of Buck Lake and its surrounding area, opting instead to make my own. As the years went by, I added islands, rivers, and new lakes to an expanding world of my creation. I discovered a "New World" in nearby Fox Lake, christened islands with names like Royal Britannia and Raymond Island (after my grandfather), and even touched off a canoe war with my neighbours. Over time, traditions were developed that included flags, medals, and epic histories.

Later, I attended Wilfrid Laurier University, publishing the history of my little world, which I had called "Mainland," in an effort to preserve it indefinitely. I meticulously gathered everything together with the help of Professor Susan Scott of the Department of Religion and Culture. Susan and I would meet over tea at her home in Waterloo as she gently guided me through the passages and portages of recording personal history.

One day, as we approached what I thought was the end of the process, Susan asked me a question that changed my entire view of this world I had claimed as my own. "Nathan," she asked, smiling at me with her hand covering her cup of tea as wisps of steam escaped through her fingers, "how are you going to handle the ideas of imperialism woven into your story?"

I could feel my canoe grinding against an unseen rock in the water.

Susan was merely enquiring about something that should have stood out as obvious to me: I had not just created my own world; I had conjured up an empire. I had projected my own identity onto the landscape of Buck Lake, and by doing so had displaced histories that had been laid down before I arrived. The very idea that other people existed on the lake and had their own worlds — just as personal and intimate — had never occurred to me.

Eventually, a new book emerged, entitled *Beyond Mainland*, in which I confessed, "I heard other names attached to the islands, rivers, and lakes that seemed so familiar to me. I was scared of those names — their existence implied a loss of control, that I was not the only steward of Buck Lake."[2] I eventually learned to relax my grip and expand my view of the land and its history, accepting that many people had travelled these same waters. It was then that I first encountered the stories of Indigenous peoples of the lake and its lands. I learned that "my" lake was part of a long chain of lakes that stretched from Georgian Bay into the eastern hinterlands of present-day Muskoka, and that this chain had once served as an important transportation route and source of food for the Indigenous peoples of the region. The place I knew as the sleepy hamlet of Ilfracombe, at the foot of Buck Lake, had been visited for centuries by the Anishinaabe.

As a boy, I had never imagined Indigenous peoples living on the lands and in the waters surrounding my cottage. I had always pictured "Indians" as being from some ancient past, far removed from my life. In school, Indigenous peoples occupied the first few pages of our history textbooks before vanishing into the mists of a long timeline. Later, when I became a teacher of Canadian history, I was very tentative about exploring the place of Indigenous peoples in that history with my students. Resources were scarce and the curriculum did not ask us to dwell too much on the subject (fortunately, that has changed in Ontario).[3] The history of the Indigenous peoples of Canada mystified me; it was filled with names that were difficult to pronounce and an oral tradition that didn't fit well with my profession's book-centred, Euro-centric focus, or its linear approach to time. If I had to admit it to myself, I was largely ignorant of the subject. What little I knew was informed by my experience of growing up during the crises in Oka and Ipperwash (not to mention the Caledonia Land Claim that erupted during my second year of teaching). I remember the media reporting on those events with little context, fueling family discussions back home that were laced with misinformation and learned racism. Growing up in Canada, my only points of contact with Indigenous peoples were the moments of conflict that occasionally occurred, which were marked by newspapers decorated with images of Natives in bandanas or behind barricades. It never occurred to me to ask why these events were happening, or question how they were being discussed in Canada. When I became an adult, it was easier to ignore the Indigenous peoples than try and make sense of what had happened between our two peoples.

My views have changed considerably since those early days as a teacher. As my previous two books (*Canada's Constitutional Monarchy* and *Prince Edward, Duke of Kent: Father of the Canadian Crown*) attest, for the past number of years I have been exploring the Crown in this country. It was through this exploration that I encountered King George III's Royal Proclamation of 1763, reading that it was the "Magna Carta" for Indigenous peoples living with Canada — an assertion repeated throughout the few resources available to me. I began to realize that the Crown was at the heart of Canada's relationship with First Nations. When the settlers and First Nations first came together to construct a delicate balance (represented so well by artist Alex MacKay's *Treaty Canoe*) that would allow them to live together on the land, the Dignified Crown became the medium through which First Nations could communicate with non-Indigenous settlers.

Through my involvement with Friends of the Canadian Crown, now the Institute for the Study of the Crown in Canada at Massey College,[4] I attended the Diamond Jubilee Conference on the Crown, held in Regina, Saskatchewan, as a discussant in October, 2012.[5] This conference began to broaden my understanding of the complex relationship that has grown between the Crown and First Nations. Talks delivered by J.R. (Jim) Miller (Canada Research Chair in Native-Newcomer Relations and professor of history at the University of Saskatchewan) and Stephanie Danyluk (a research analyst in the Department of Self-Government at Whitecap Dakota First Nation) introduced me to the ancient practice of First Nations making European monarchs, and thus their subjects, kin. As J.R. Miller explained to the attendees:

> Kinship and alliance are the heart of the ties to the Crown. Understanding these ties allows us to appreciate where we as a country have gone wrong in the past and, perhaps, to discern how we might improve relations in the future.[6]

In his 2014 discussion on the place of Indigenous concepts of love in Canada's Constitution for the CBC Radio One program *Ideas*, Professor John Borrows (Professor of Law at both the University of Minnesota Law School and the University of Victoria) spoke of how love was woven into the treaties.

"When Indigenous peoples signed treaties with the Crown in Canada," Borrows explained, "love was frequently invoked, even in the face of sharp disagreements."[7]

During the September 2013 opening in Vancouver of the Truth and Reconciliation Commission (the commission established in 2008 in the aftermath of Canada's Indian Residential School System), the chair, Justice Murray Sinclair, remarked, "For the survivors [of Indian Residential Schools] in this room the most important gesture of reconciliation that they will ever see in their lives is for you to tell them that you love them."[8]

It is here that language must be explored. Language is the atmosphere in which we live and see the world around us — that I think and write this in English immediately puts me at a disadvantage when speaking of another people. English Canadians are familiar with the issues raised by different groups speaking different languages as a result of their sometimes strained relationship with their French-speaking sisters and brothers. However, even though French and English are different forms of expression, they are rooted in a similar European tradition. There are shared experiences embracing religion, philosophy, and culture that allow their different worlds to make some sort of sense to each other.

With a common Judeo-Christian background, the Europeans who landed on this continent over the past five hundred years have shared a relationship with the environment that has deep biblical roots. Much can be gleaned about how European Canadians understand their connection to the land by reading Genesis 1:26 (New International Version): "Then God said, 'Let us make mankind in our image, in our likeness, so that they may rule over the fish in the sea and the birds in the sky, over the livestock and all the wild animals, and over all the creatures that move along the ground.'" Later, in verse 28, God is quoted as saying, "Be fruitful and increase in number; fill the earth and subdue it. Rule over the fish in the sea and the birds in the sky and over every living creature that moves on the ground."

The use of words such as *rule*, sometimes translated as *dominion*, and *subdue* (originally written in Hebrew, and later Latin, before being translated into the common languages of Europe) create power dynamics between humans (made in the image of God) and the environment.

Even though modern Canadian society is secular, with a clear separation between religion and the state, we cannot ignore the fact that the languages of those who migrated from Europe to these shores are the products of a Judeo-Christian world.

First Nation languages share no genes with those languages that are the products of the European concept of the world. As an example, 70 percent of Anishinaabemowin (the Anishinaabe language) is comprised of verbs — a much greater percentage than is found in any European language (English has approximately 12.5 percent in the spoken language).[9] The extensive use of analogy and metaphor, as opposed to the more common use of direct references and explanations employed by European languages, can be found throughout Indigenous communities (both historic and present-day). Anishinaabe names for places and landmarks typically reflect their relationship with them, or the location's place in relation to the surrounding environment (For example: Toronto's Humber River was originally called *Cobechenonk*, meaning "leave the canoes and go back.") This style of naming contrasts with the European habit of designating features of the environment after significant people, places, or events.

I can offer another, specifically English, example of the problem created by language, by continuing John Borrows's exploration of the word *love*. In English, we only have this one word to explain a very complex and powerful experience. In my own life I throw the word *love* around repeatedly: I love my wife; I love my family; I love my students; I love my morning coffee. All of these relationships are different, and yet I only have one word that conveys an emotional connection that I am trying to get across. Other English-speakers understand that I am not applying the same definition of "love" to my wife as I do my morning coffee, even though I am not giving them any other verbs to work with.

Bruce Morito addresses this idea in the introduction to his book *An Ethic of Mutual Respect: The Covenant Chain and Aboriginal-Crown Relations* when he cites Clifford Geertz's notion of the "rich descriptor." Morito explains "… where rich descriptors are used for purposes of communication, we can conclude that the people who use them appropriately presuppose a rich array of supporting and contributing intangible factors."[10] Love is a rich descriptor, but other English-speakers appreciate that and graft their experiences and relationships onto mine, thereby understanding that my love for coffee is not familial.

Move into other cultures, however, and different words have been developed to provide names for the many "love" relationships we can have — I immediately think of the Greek concept of "*agape*," or the word "*mettā*" from ancient India. These words are vaguely translatable into English, but their essences are not. If those languages were to die, the distinctions and experiences those words evoke would die with them.

The gap in meaning between languages described above exists between European languages and First Nations languages. As a result, one would imagine that attempts at settler/First Nations communication would be bound to fail as the worlds created by these very different realities are largely untranslatable. Paradoxically, Professor Morito offers a counter-argument: the lack of rich descriptors and the nuances in Indigenous languages that are found in English and other European languages may actually have led to a deeper relationship between the settlers and the Indigenous peoples because it necessitated careful listening and exploration of each other's experiences. Morito explains, "the First Nation/Crown treaty relationship turned out to be deeper … precisely because both parties had to dig deeply into their imaginations and capacities to develop a shared lifeworld that people of the same culture would have [had], because they [took] so much for granted."[11]

The referencing of Queen Victoria as "The Great White Mother," or of King George III as "Father," is famous in Indigenous history, and at the beginning was understood to invoke a strong relationship of equality. However, the meaning behind these rich descriptors has been lost, or deliberately corrupted, over time. When we look specifically at Anishinaabe culture and family structure, the problem with trying to explain relationships between radically different cultures becomes apparent.

Seventeenth- and eighteenth-century Anishinaabe culture was very anti-hierarchical, with no concept of a paramount chief — any demonstrations of selfishness or ego was abhorred. Professor Evans Dowd, explaining the Odawa Nation in his book *War under Heaven*, writes, "To call leadership decentralized in these societies is almost to miss the point, because centralization was not an issue … Indian leadership was not authoritarian."[12] Dowd explains that the Odawa term for a civil leader was *ogema*, i.e., a highly respected man who headed a network of extended families but held no authority to impose his opinions on others. Dowd writes, "The ideal [Odawa] leader forged alliances through displays of generosity. He was composed, dependable, and willing to withstand long hours of negotiation. He mediated disputes among his followers and between his followers and others. He received gifts and redistributed them to his people; likewise, he gathered gifts from his people and gave these, in exchanges, to others."[13] The very idea of a leader in the community was markedly different from that of the Europeans whom they were encountering. This is especially true of women in Indigenous societies, who are often the glue that holds everything together — the "backbone of the Nation," I am often told.

It was with words used to describe family relationships that Europeans and First Nations began to sort out their interactions with one another. The problem that immediately emerged was that the meanings of the words — different depending on the language and culture employing them — bore little resemblance to the relationship they were intended to explain. The Anishinaabe concept of fatherhood, an equal relationship within the family that involved protection and generosity, bore no resemblance to its European counterpart, which was based in a male-dominated, hierarchical society.

In her exploration of the relationship between the Dignified Crown and western Canada during the nineteenth century, the University of Calgary's Sarah Carter explains:

… while the addresses that successive governors general delivered to First Nations, replete with references to the Great Mother (Queen Victoria) and her "red children," spoke of inequality rather than equality from the perspective of the vice-regal visitor, this was not how they were received by First Nations, who heard powerful affirmations of their familial relationship.[14]

As Carter reminds her readers, referencing the Crown as "Mother" or "Father" was not an act of submission; instead, it was a declaration by an Indigenous Nation that they were equal members of the same family as their "brothers," the British subjects they were encountering in their territory. Modern instances of such familial names being conferred on the Monarch, or their representatives, include the Salish Nation bestowing the name "Mother of All People" on Queen Elizabeth II in 1959, and the Kainai Nation (Blood Tribe) conferring a chieftainship on Governor General Adrienne Clarkson as "Grandmother of Many Nations" in 2005.

At the beginning of their interactions with Indigenous peoples in North America, Europeans "got it," and employed these terms while meeting with their new partners. An interesting account survives from 1815, when a Hudson's Bay Company surveyor characterized King George III as the "Great Father of us all" in his efforts to secure peaceful relations with the Nations near the Red River Settlement.[15] This reference was taken by the Nēhiraw (Cree) and Saulteaux peoples as a metaphor denoting equality — that the HBC and their rivals, the North West Company, were both children of the Great Father (king). Such an understanding was affirmed during the 1817 Selkirk Treaty.

Sir William Johnson (superintendent of Indian Affairs for the northern colonies, 1756–1774) deliberately referred to Indigenous allies as "Brothers" and the King as "Father" (presumably in an Indigenous context). Even as late as 1876, Alexander Morris, the lieutenant governor of the North-West Territories, greeted delegates from the Nēhiraw Nations assembled outside Fort Carlton (in present-day Saskatchewan) saying:

> What I say and what you say, and what we do, is done openly before the whole people. You are, like me and my friends who are with me, *children of the Queen* [author's emphasis]. We are of the same blood, the same God made us and the same Queen rules over us. I am a Queen's Councillor, I am her Governor of all these territories, and I am here to speak from her to you…. I have been nearly four years Governor of Manitoba and these territories, and from the day I was sworn, *I took the Indian by the hand, and those who took it have never let go….*[16]

However, while his rhetoric seems to respect the equality enshrined in the Treaty of Niagara and Covenant Chain, Morris slides in a phrase that would have turned Johnson's blood cold. Seemingly affirming the equality of the Nēhiraw with the European settlers, Morris defines it by saying " … you are subjects of the Queen as I am. She cares as much for one of you as she does for one of her white subjects."[17]

If all peoples are equal only as subjects of the Monarch in this country, a problem emerges: Canada's constitutional set-up separates the *Efficient* from the *Dignified* Crown and expects the Queen, or her representatives, to act on the advice of a democratically elected government. Canadian legislatures use representation by population — a practice that dooms First Nations, whose lands have been flooded with waves of non-Indigenous immigrants. While what Alexander Morris is saying sounds nice, peppered as it is with references to an active "Great White Mother," the Canadian Constitution did not allow for the sort of relationship he describes to exist.

Publishing *The Treaties of Canada with the Indians of Manitoba and the North-West Territories* in 1880, Morris offered another nudge to the relationship between the Crown and First Nations when he wrote in his conclusion "The Future of the Indians":

Alexander Morris, lieutenant governor of the North-West Territories from 1872–1876. Throughout his career, and on behalf of the Crown, Morris signed Treaties Three, Four, Five, and Six. *William James Topley/Library and Archives Canada/PA-025469.*

They are wards of Canada, let us do our duty by them, and repeat in the North-West, the success which has attended our dealings with them in old Canada, for the last hundred years … let us have a wise and paternal Government carrying out the provisions of our treaties, and doing its utmost to help and elevate the Indian population, who have been cast upon our care.…

Morris's final statement captures the new, paternalistic relationship that had begun to overshadow the Covenant Chain. The equality demanded by the Treaty of Niagara was replaced by a new relationship, where First Nations were seen as wards of the Crown. The lieutenant governor concluded:

… instead of the Indian melting away, as one of them in older Canada tersely put it, "as snow before the sun," we will see our Indian population, loyal subjects of the Crown, happy, prosperous, and self-sustaining, and Canada will be enabled to feel, that in a truly patriotic spirit, our country has done its duty by the red men of the North-West, and thereby to herself. So may it be.[18]

European-rich descriptors of the family dynamic were now being imposed on the relationships between the Crown (deliberately being presented by colonial officials as the Efficient and Dignified dimensions fused together) and First Nations. Attributes of the Crown including generosity and dependability, with no ability to impose on other members of the family, were replaced with concepts of benevolent authoritarianism and subjugation by colonial officials, who co-opted these relationships and remoulded them to suit long-term goals of assimilation. It is these mid-nineteenth-century definitions of relationship that have formed the collective narrative of Canada — they have become the lens through which many non-Indigenous Canadians see First Nations today.

As settlers flooded west across the great plains, treaty commissioners presented themselves as direct representatives of the Queen, the "Great

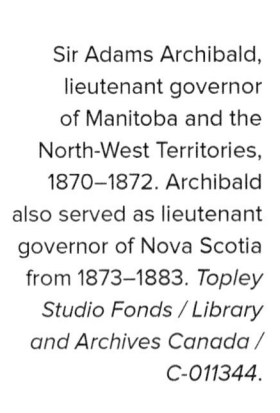

Sir Adams Archibald, lieutenant governor of Manitoba and the North-West Territories, 1870–1872. Archibald also served as lieutenant governor of Nova Scotia from 1873–1883. *Topley Studio Fonds / Library and Archives Canada / C-011344.*

White Mother," fostering the familial relationship in order to get the land they needed for European settlement. The shift from a relationship based on equality to that of submission can also be seen in Lieutenant Governor Adams Archibald's address at the Council of Treaty One: "Your Great Mother wishes the good of all races under her sway. She wishes her red children to be happy and contented. She wishes them to live in comfort."

It should be noted that by these words Archibald had made another slight adjustment to the role of the Crown in its Treaty relationship. Instead of the Crown offering protection, the lieutenant governor has substituted that word with "sway," or influence. The Queen's representative goes on to say, "She would like them to adopt the habits of the whites, to till the land and raise food and store it up against a time of want."[19]

This new role for the Queen further eclipses the traditional (and was never intended by the ancient Covenant Chain relationship). Echoing the relationship articulated by Alexander Morris, Archibald used the "Great White Mother" to give instructions to First Nations — supplanting the original Treaty dynamic with a European one of a parent to a child. As Peter Carstens explains in his preface to *The Queen's People*, "It is therefore a mockery of that trust that from the colonial period onwards the lawmakers and administrators set in authority over [N]ative peoples of Canada were also the Queen's people."[20]

By pulling the interpretation of the Crown/First Nation relationship fully into the English language, the horrors of Canada's Indian Residential School System seem inevitable. The extinction of Indigenous worlds, including their ancient relationship with the Queen, required the destruction of Indigenous ways of explaining it to themselves and others. Native languages had to be eradicated, and children separated from the older generations. If Indigenous peoples lost the words and stories they used to describe their relationships with one another, as well as the Queen, their assimilation would be complete because they would become mute — only European understandings and definitions would remain.

When treaties are seen only through the lens of a European language, they are reduced simply to contracts rather than the living familial relationships they were intended to be (for First Nations "treaty" is a verb, not a noun). As Bruce Morito explains:

> Understanding the lifeworld or mindset of one's allies could only be accomplished to a certain degree, partly because of psychological limitations in the human capacity to make foreign cultures intelligible without knowing the other's language. Both parties would have lacked the ability … to detect and automatically interpret nuances in the behaviour and speech of others.[21]

The difference between breaking a contract (an action associated with a penalty such as a fine) and breaking a Treaty (the destruction of a family relationship) is dramatic and demands a more thorough understanding by Canadians.

While exploring language and relationships, it is also important to acknowledge the differences between written and oral histories, and their effect on the concept of time. European history has a tradition of being written, and is often presented on a timeline. By assigning dates to various events and the people who participated in them, a sense of distance is immediately created between the historical incident and the present-day — between then and now. History becomes a series of events, each building off the next, giving the impression of a "progression" into the future. "Moving forward" is always seen as better, synonymous with progress. One consequence of such a view of history is that the present supersedes the past, with the effect that the past inevitably becomes diminished.

Oral history is different. Dates are irrelevant, as history becomes a story that encompasses the listener. The 1996 Royal Commission on Aboriginal Peoples explained:

Unlike the western scientific tradition, which creates a sense of distance in time between the listener or reader and the events being described, the tendency of Aboriginal perspectives is to create a sense of immediacy by encouraging listeners to imagine that they are participating in the past event being recounted. Ideas about how the universe was created offer a particularly compelling example of differences in approach to interpreting the past.[22]

A European worldview plants a Treaty on a timeline that we are constantly moving away from. Treaties become static things that can fall into abeyance or even become obsolete if enough time passes. For the historian, a Treaty becomes an artifact, insulated from the reader by the passage of time. Written text is frozen — a one-way conversation that becomes harder and harder to relate to since it cannot evolve to embrace contemporary language, which continues to develop.

In an oral tradition, words are important, and they can be explored using new terms, phrases, and analogies that have developed since the story was first spoken. Interpretation and agreement become central to the Treaty relationship, which helps explain why councils could last for days as both sides explained how they understood their relationship with each other. A tradition of consensus demands constant communication and negotiation. Daniel K. Richter explains that "[T]he process of treaty making was always far more important to Indians than the results enshrined in a treaty document."[23]

As with time, treaties are meant to be a continuing "work in progress" — they are never finished — *that* is the point. Treaties demand that both parties meet regularly to recite the words and stories associated with their relationship to one another, reinterpreting them and consensually agreeing to live together anew. Disagreements must be talked through. This is why love is so important to the Treaty relationship. Disagreements between family members can be visceral, even downright ugly, but as long as the parties involved love each other (and this does not mean they have to like one another), there will always be hope for compromise and consensus.

I once heard from an Indigenous negotiator that Canada deals with modern Treaty negotiations as if they were divorce proceedings; lawyers are involved as details are hammered out in some sort of agreement that will settle things once and for all, so that both sides can move on separately with their lives. An Indigenous perspective sees treaties as a marriage: a relationship that is constantly evolving. Filled with agreement and disagreement, times of intense love and cold distance, a marriage is always a work in progress. Never static, it is a relationship that requires constant communication, attention, and respect. As with any successful marriage, love must always be found at its centre.

When Indigenous peoples speak of their relationship with the Crown, it should not be taken simply as something that was created in the past. Canadian conceptions of the Crown see it as a constantly evolving institution on a timeline, moving forward into the unknown future. Our Constitution allows for powers unused by the Crown to die through the passage of time — a "use it or lose it" principle. The powers and concept of the eighteenth-century Crown in Canada are dramatically different from those of the twenty-first-century one. Looking at the Crown using a First Nation perspective and concept of time presents a dramatically different institution. The promises and relationship agreed to in Treaty are as important and relevant today as they were when first negotiated. What we have in Canada is a perception problem concerning the Crown that needs to be revisited by all parties involved. By just looking at the different concepts of time involved, the complexity of this task becomes strikingly apparent.

Early into my teaching career I visited the epicentre of Canada's Indian Residential School System, the Mohawk Institute in Brantford, Ontario. Created as a residential school in 1828, the "Mush Hole" (as it was called by those that were made to attend) began the devastating effort by the Canadian government to "kill the Indian in the child," or as Duncan Campbell Scott, deputy superintendent of Indian Affairs, articulated in 1920, "... to get rid of the Indian Problem.... Our object is to continue until there is not a single Indian in Canada that has not been absorbed into the body politic...."[24]

Thinking about that visit today brings to mind Thomas King's remarkable Massey Lecture series, The Truth About Stories. After speaking about being abandoned by his father and raised by his mother, King reminded his audience, "I tell the stories not to play on your sympathies but to suggest how stories can control our lives, for there is a part of me that has never been able to move past these stories, a part of me that will be chained to these stories as long as I live."

Learning about Canada's attempt to wipe out Indigenous identity and culture in this land is a story that many non-Indigenous Canadians are hearing for the first time. The rawness of this period serves to keep

After receiving the Covenant Chain Wampum replica from Ken Maracle, my wife and I visited the "Mush Hole" in Brantford, Ontario. This residential school operated from 1828 until 1970, when it was closed. The building and property were then turned over to the Six Nations of the Grand River. Canada's last federally operated residential school (Gordon Residential School near Punnichy, Saskatchewan) was closed in 1996. *Courtesy of author.*

the wounds open and festering. For many, seeing Canada as a place capable of such acts is uncomfortable — even unimaginable. As Thomas King said, "… once a story is told, it cannot be called back. Once told, it is loose in the world."[25]

People who had once referred to Europeans as kin had thousands of their children removed from their mothers and grandmothers and forcibly assimilated into a culture that had originally pledged to follow agreements such as the *Teioháte Kaswenta*, or Two-Row Wampum. The abuse inflicted for over a century poisoned a relationship that was originally founded in equality, and corrupted it into one of rape, torture, and murder.

Thanks to such organizations as the Truth and Reconciliation Commission, the stories circling around the hundreds of residential school sites in this country are loose in the world. So it must be. Stories such as these need to be chained to this country's history, recognized as a part of our collective journey together. Such a step is key to the future of Canada, if we are, in the words of the Honourable Steven L. Point, ever to "paddle together in the same canoe."

Residential schools remain the most dramatic example in the breakdown of Canada's relationship with First Nations, but there are many other indignities that have been suffered. Exploring Prime Minister Stephen Harper's 2008 apology to the victims of residential schools, Eva MacKay quotes Michael Doxtater in *The Apologizer's Apology* saying, "The closing of the residential school door leads down a hallway with other doors most Indians know about. The partnership now involves walking down that hallway together."[26]

This has not simply been the collapse of a political alliance, or the breach of a contract from long ago. What happened in Canada was the breakdown of complex familial relationships between the Crown and Indigenous peoples. If it were simply a European-style contractual agreement that had been broken — like a pre-nuptial agreement — the solution would be relatively simple, albeit costly. However, these were relationships grounded in love — a word with no concrete definition in English (and certainly not one that finds harmony with Indigenous conceptions). For centuries we tried to relate to one another in Treaty, and the Dignified Crown (an institution rooted in honour, tradition, dependability, and consistency) provided non-Indigenous peoples with a way to communicate. However, it was the Europeans that changed the dynamic.

Professor Dowd saw signs of this change after the Seven Years War (1754–1763), writing that "… language was critical to the failure of the British and Indians to establish a working relationship" after the French Crown had been expelled from the Great Lakes watershed, even citing Shawnees referencing the English's "evil speech."[27] In the eyes of the First Nations across this continent, evil speech festered to the point where the settler population, under the Indian Residential School System, took Indigenous children from their parents and began systematically deconstructing their cultures. As I wrote earlier, one of the prime targets in that effort was the complete eradication of Indigenous languages.

The logic is sound: If the intent is to destroy the worldview of another people, the very words they use to express their reality and define their relationships must be obliterated. If no words are left to describe an experience, it ceases to exist. With Indigenous languages extinguished, First Nations would be forced to embrace European words and the concepts they express. Put simply, if First Nations did not have words for subjugation and ownership, they needed to be forced into a language that did. It should be no wonder that Justice Murray Sinclair, addressing students at the University of Manitoba on February 16, 2012, characterized what happened in Canada's Indian Residential School System as meeting the requirements of the United Nation's definition of genocide.[28]

For the 150th anniversary of the Charlottetown Conference, Stephen Lewis (often described as Canada's most respected citizen) was awarded a prestigious Symons Medal and asked to deliver a lecture on the state of Confederation. Addressing his audience gathered in Charlottetown,

Prince Edward Island, Lewis (an honorary witness of the Truth and Reconciliation Commission) characterized the contemporary landscape for First Nations as racist.

"Sure, there was an apology," Lewis acknowledged, "but an apology is ultimately gratuitous, ultimately self-serving and devious if it's not accompanied by root and branch educational reform."[29]

CHAPTER TWO

# The 1764 Treaty of Niagara and Covenant Chain of Friendship

*You have now been here for several days, during which time we have frequently met to Renew, and strengthen our Engagements, & you have made so many Promises of your Friendship, and Attachment to the English that there now only remains for us to exchange the great Belt of the Covenant Chain that we may not forget our mutual Engagements*

Sir William Johnson, Niagara, 1764

Sir William Johnson, superintendent of Indian Affairs for the northern colonies (1756–1774), ca. 1760. *Artist unknown. Library and Archives Canada, Acc. No. 1989-407-X.*

In the fall of 2013, the Indigenous Bar Association held its annual general meeting with the theme, "Peace, Friendship and Respect: A Critical Examination of the Honour of the Crown on the 250th Anniversary of the Royal Proclamation and the Treaty of Niagara."

Hosted by Rama First Nation, the conference included a commemoration ceremony for the 250th anniversary of the Royal Proclamation on October 7.

Issued by King George III, the Royal Proclamation of 1763 was the British government's reorganization of European North America after the defeat of the French Crown during the 1754–1763 Beaver Wars (called the Seven Years War in Europe, and the French and Indian Wars by the American and French colonists). The majority of the proclamation dealt with the management of the newly acquired French territories and the distribution of land for officers and soldiers who fought for the British Crown. However, in the final third of the document the "Indians" are addressed:

> ... it is just and reasonable, and essential to our Interest, and the Security of our Colonies, that the several Nations or Tribes of Indians with whom We are connected, and who live under our Protection, should not be molested or disturbed in the Possession of such Parts of Our Dominions and Territories as, not having been ceded to or purchased by Us, are reserved to them, or any of them, as their Hunting Grounds.[1]

That the King refers to Indigenous peoples as comprising "Nations" is significant, as is his affirmation of a connection to them. It is for these reasons that the Royal Proclamation is often held up as legitimizing Indigenous ownership of the land. Of course, this assertion requires us to believe that First Nations needed the Monarch of a far-off land to tell them that they owned the land they had inhabited for millennia. It should also be noted that the criteria used to place First Nations under the King's protection established a formula through which they could be divested of their territories (by ceding or selling them to the Crown). While sovereignty was implicitly granted to the Indigenous Nations of British North America, it fell within the parameters of a definition that required European acknowledgement to exist.

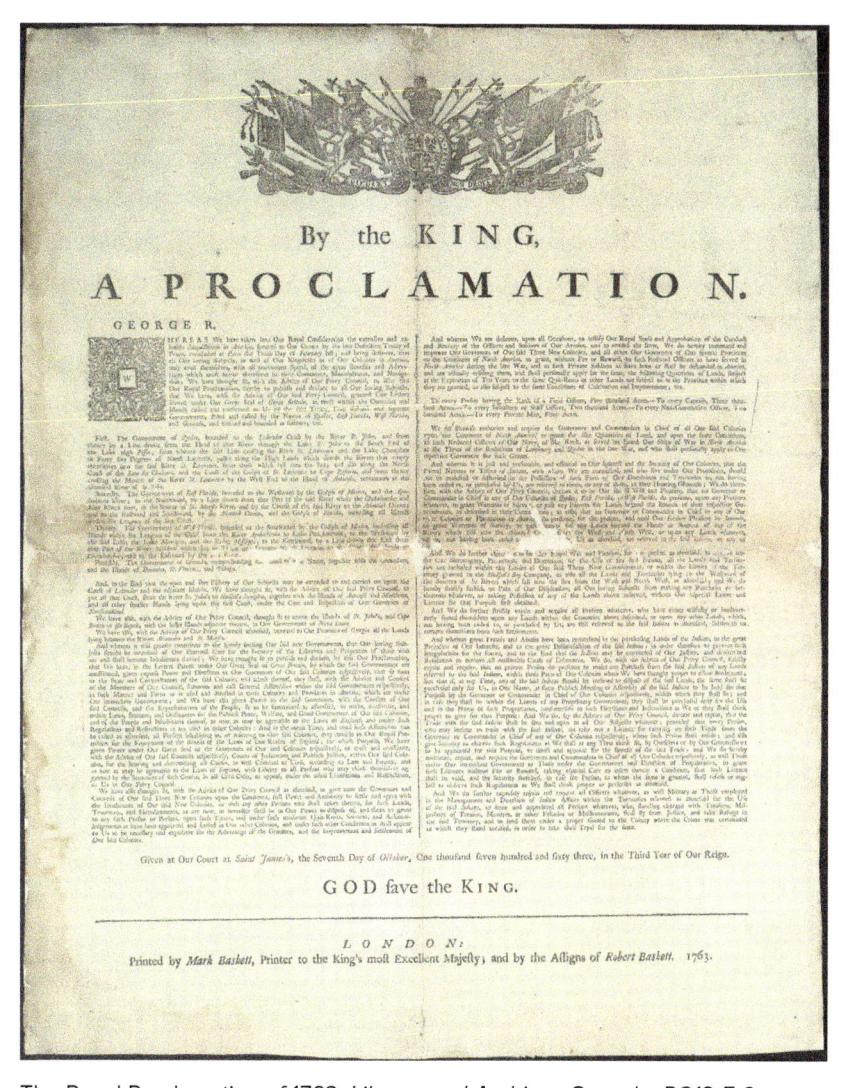

The Royal Proclamation of 1763. *Library and Archives Canada, RG13-F-6.*

A variety of presentations were made to the group that gathered at Rama First Nation to acknowledge the Royal Proclamation, including an address by Justice Murray Sinclair, and a reading of the wampum exchanged at Niagara (including a replica of the 1764 Covenant Chain Wampum) offered by Alan Corbiere of M'Chigeeng First Nation.

While First Nations did not see the need to write down their languages, this does not mean that they did not have documents to record significant events. Wampum — objects woven using sinew and white and purple beads made from quahog, a mollusk whose shells are found along the northeastern coast of North America — are sacred diplomatic devices, used to represent agreements and relationships, facilitating communication between Nations across much of Turtle Island. As J.R. Miller explains in *Compact, Contract, Covenant: Aboriginal Treaty-Making in Canada*:

> Wampum … was a mnemonic, or memory assisting device, a First Nations' archives in effect. Wampum recorded important discussions and agreements between [N]ations, especially matters of peace and war. At subsequent councils, [an Indigenous] speaker would remind the other party [of] the agreement by reading the wampum, that is, holding up the belt that commemorated the pact and going through the terms of the understanding between the parties that were recorded on the [w]ampum "document."[2]

Alan Corbiere explained in his article "Their Own Forms of Which They Take the Most Notice" that "The symbols woven onto Wampum belts were designed to convey specific meanings on specific belts, and the oral tradition ensured that this meaning was preserved and maintained."[3] Not only a mnemonic device, wampum sealed any agreements or meetings — it was a sacred act that was required in order for any Treaty or important event to be legitimate.

That night in Rama First Nation the wampum exchanged at Niagara in 1764 were read, and the assembled guests were reminded of what had been recorded within them.

I must confess that I went to this gathering with the idea that the focus of the evening would be on the Royal Proclamation — "Canada's Indian Magna Carta,"[4] as it has been called — and that the Crown would be affirmed as a protector of First Nation's rights with this document as ground zero of the relationship. This thought was quickly dismissed.

"I love the Royal Proclamation," Justice Murray Sinclair confessed that night, "and hate it at the same time."[5]

Justice Sinclair explained that, at best, King George's proclamation was an imposed relationship by a far-away and aloof government focused on protecting its trading relationships. At worst, the document created the framework that allowed Indigenous title to be extinguished and Indigenous lands to be transferred to the settler population.

According to Corbiere's reading of the wampum exchanged at the Council of Niagara one year after George III's Royal Proclamation, it was not until after the Treaty of Niagara was concluded that the King's words, agreed to after intense negotiations, became relevant to the assembled Western Nations. To put it simply: the Royal Proclamation was fully rejected by the Western Nations as a stand-alone document. John Borrows wrote in his Ph.D. thesis that the Treaty of Niagara revealed what was "hidden in the Royal Proclamation's words."[6]

Before the great assembly at *the crooked place* (Niagara), Pontiac's War (1763–1766) had evicted British soldiers from forts across the western frontier of old New France. The British Crown was trying to project its sovereignty over the vast North American continent, but peace had never been separately concluded with the Indigenous allies of the French Crown. The King's representative, Governor General Jeffery Amherst, did not want Indigenous peoples to get in the way of British interests northwest of the Hudson River, despite promises made to the contrary under the Articles of Capitulation he had signed at Montreal with the French governor general, the Marquis de Vaudreuil. Article 40 of the capitulation recognized the independence of the Anishinaabe and Wendat allies of the French, guaranteeing that they "shall be maintained in the Lands they inhabit, if they chose to remain there … [and] they shall not be molested on any pretense whatsoever."

Amherst immediately pursued policies that antagonized the Nations gathered around the Great Lakes watershed that had once been, and in many cases still remained, bound to the King of France.[7] One of the first acts of the principal representative of the British Crown in North America, a man who "radiated contempt for Indians,"[8] was to reduce the number of gifts exchanged with the First Nations each year.

Gift-giving was (and remains) an integral part of Indigenous diplomacy in the region — characterized by some as a display of "love" between the British and their allies. Recalling the central role generosity played (and plays) in ideals of leadership in Indigenous society and family, the importance of gift-giving (which was seen as an act of renewing relationship) cannot be downplayed. Professor Dowd, author of *War Under Heaven*, explains that Amherst was "… determined to invest gifts, key symbols of the empire's Indian relations, with new meanings. Gifts might still occasionally be given to Indians, but they [were] not to be [the] gifts of the grateful to the benefactor … rather, they were to be the charity of the gentry to the beggar."[9] Some colonial officials began referring to their Indigenous allies as subjects of the King, or "children" (a term imbued with European connotations of subjugation to a dominant parent, not the freedom and independence assigned to them by Indigenous languages).

Sir William Johnson, proficient in Indigenous protocol, warned Amherst that his approach would only antagonize the Western Nations. An Irishman by birth, Johnson could sympathize with Indigenous anxieties over English expansionism. Amherst baulked at Johnson's advice, confident that his military presence in the area would be able to control the Indigenous population. He was gravely mistaken.

Odawa Chief Pontiac led a loose alliance of Anishinaabe and Seneca warriors that saw nearly every one of the forts surrounding the Great Lakes burned to the ground (Fort Michilimackinac famously succumbed to a siege that began with a game of *baaga'adowe* — a forerunner of modern lacrosse[10] — between Ojibwe and Sauks). Forts Detroit, Pitt, and Niagara were also besieged until Sir William's policy of building relationships finally prevailed over Amherst's attempts to project British sovereignty. Amherst was recalled to England in disgrace; an imposed relationship would not do.

While military outposts smouldered across the interior of the continent, Sir William Johnson argued that Indigenous diplomacy would have to be employed in order to have King George's contentious proclamation ratified. The sometimes erratic Royal Proclamation, (implying First Nations sovereignty in some places, while denying it in others) needed to be made explicit using Indigenous frameworks and perspectives.[11] For First Nations, the written document would always come second to how it would be verbally explained and defined.

Discussing an appropriate location for a Great Council that would encompass the Western Nations of the Great Lakes, Sir William wrote a letter to Thomas Gage (Jeffery Amherst's replacement as commander of the British Forces in North America) dated February 19, 1764, saying:

> I Judged it too great a Compliment to treat with the Indians in their own Country, indeed was it not for the Expense of bringing them down, it would be probably best to treat with them here [at Johnson Hall, Sir William's residence], as they all consider this place as their Grand *Fireplace* for Treaty's of that Nature; but I am induced to think that *Oswego*, or *Niagara* would answer very well, because great part of the Chipeweighs, & Missassagas, live on the North sides of Lakes Ontario & Erie to which Niagara would serve as a Centre without being too distant for those who live in the Neighbourhood of Detroit & if we treat with the Chenussios, or any of that Quarter (which may probably be the case) no place can be better calculated.

Sir William's refusal to meet with the Western Nations "in their Own Country" should be noted. Johnson goes on to write:

At this Treaty wheresoever held we should tye them down (in the peace) according to their own forms of which they take the most notice, for Example by Exchanging a very large belt with some remarkable & intelligible figures thereon. Expressive of the occasion which should be always shewn at public Meetings, to remind them of their promises; and that we should Exchange Articles with the Signatures of the Chiefs of every Tribe; The use of frequent Meetings with Indians is here pointed out. They want the use of letters, consequently they must frequently be reminded of their promises, & this custom they keep up Strictly, amongst themselves, since the neglect of the one, will prove a breach of the other.[12]

The last line is an important one, reminding Gage that Indigenous diplomacy — including the use of wampum — must be married with British practices in order for something like the Royal Proclamation, and peace along the northwestern frontier, to be successful. Written words were meaningless unless they were spoken anew at regular meetings, reminding the Treaty partners of their responsibilities. Sir William readily admits in his letter to Gage that a request "that every Nation for the future shall on our requisition [be] properly made [to] deliver up, such of their people as may be guilty of Robbery or Murder, that they may be tried according to the English Laws" violated the Covenant Chain (originally made with the Haudenosaunee and discussed later in this chapter) and would be a hard one to negotiate.[13] Sir William went on to explain to the British commander-in-chief that the following assertions would need to be made to the Western Nations in order to establish a Treaty relationship:

- A free, fair and open trade;

- A free intercourse, and passage into territories under the jurisdiction of the British Crown;

- The Crown would make no Settlements or Encroachments contrary to Treaty, or without their permission;

- The Crown would bring to justice anyone who commits robbery or murders on them;

- The Crown would protect and aid them against their and our Enemies, and duly observe our Engagements with them.[14]

With the location and parameters of the discussion agreed, Sir William met with members of the Algonquin and Nipissing Nations at Oswegatchie (in modern-day New York State). Representatives from those two Nations soon fanned out across the Great Lakes region and beyond during the winter of 1763–1764 with copies of the Royal Proclamation as well as strings of wampum, inviting Nations to meet with Sir William (as a representative of the King) at Fort Niagara.[15]

### Haudenosaunee Confederacy and Nations represented at the 1764 Great Council at Niagara (the Crooked Place).[16]

(Please note that the different nations are being identified using eighteenth-century European interpretations of their names)

| Algonquins | Nippisings | Cayugas |
| Chippewas | Odawas | Conoys |
| Crees | Sacs | Mohicans |
| Fox | Toughkamiwons | Mohawks |
| Hurons | Potawatomies | Nanticokes |
| Pawnees | Cannesandagas | Onondagas |
| Menominees | Caughnawagas | Senecas[17] |

The Great Council called by Johnson met in July of 1764 outside of Fort Niagara. Over two thousand chiefs and sachems representing

THE QUEEN AT THE COUNCIL FIRE

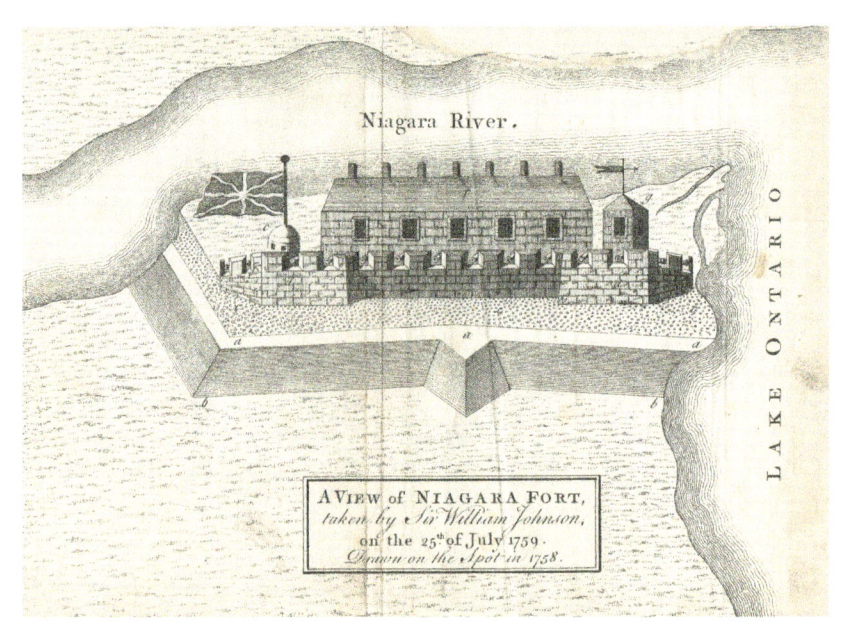

A sketch of Fort Niagara drawn on the spot by Sir William Johnson on July 25, 1759. *Courtesy of Library and Archives Canada, R11981-130-8-E.*

Fort Niagara during the commemorations of the Treaty of Niagara, August 1, 2014, 250 years after the Great Council. A feast was hosted at the fort by the Haudenosaunee and Anishinaabe nations; attended by the lieutenant governor of Ontario. *Courtesy of author.*

Some of the replica wampum on display in the Johnson Room of the French Castle at Fort Niagara the evening of the great feast of August 1, 2014. The wampum would have been laid out this way by Sir William Johnson during the Council of Niagara, 250 years earlier. *Courtesy of author.*

as many as twenty-four Nations converged on the Niagara Peninsula, the bridge of land connecting the eastern shores of Turtle Island with its centre in the northwest. Already in treaty with the Crown, the Haudenosaunee camped outside Fort Niagara (on the site where a U.S. Coast Guard base is now located), while the Anishinaabe slept on the opposite shores of the Niagara River ("Indian Country" to use Sir William's terminology).

It was at this council, using Indigenous diplomacy and traditions, including the exchange of wampum rather than written documents (Rick Hill, of the Deyohahá:ge: Indigenous Knowledge Centre, counts eighty-four separate wampum passed between the various parties[18]) that King George III's Royal Proclamation of 1763 was clarified and ratified.

The Treaty took a month to negotiate as Sir William Johnson met with each Nation separately to exchange wampum and other gifts, establishing what was to be the basis of relationship in the land. Based on

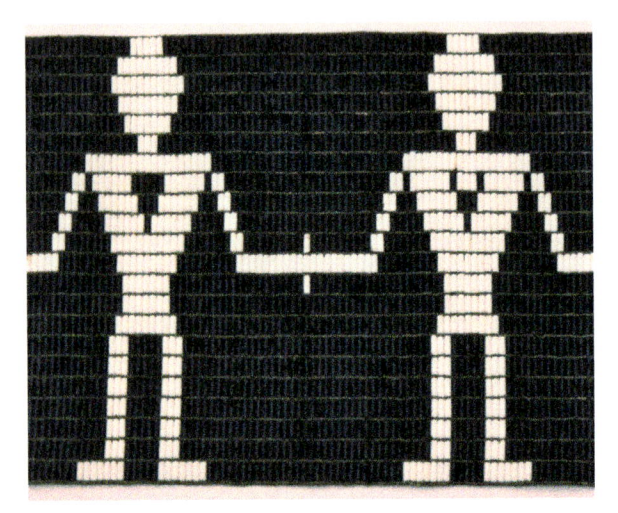

Close-up showing the central figures of the 1764 Covenant Chain Wampum representing the Crown (left) and First Nations (right). *Courtesy of author.*

the understanding that both parties — the Crown and the twenty-four assembled First Nations — were sovereign entities, a partnership based on equality was kindled. The resulting Treaty of Niagara extended the ancient Covenant Chain of Friendship north across the Niagara River to Fort Michilimackinac.

On July 29, 1764, Sir William Johnson crossed the Niagara River from Fort Niagara, leaving the eastern territories (contemporary New York State) already in relationship with the British King to land on the western shore of "Indian Country" to meet the thousands encamped there. Richard Merritt, author of *On the Commons*, believes that it was near Navy Hall, at what is now "The Commons" of Niagara-on-the-Lake, that Sir William formally concluded the Treaty through the exchange of wampum with the assembled chiefs and sachems. The first wampum presented by the Crown was described by Johnson's secretary, Captain Norman McLeod, as "… the great Covenant Chain, 23 Rows broad, & the Year 1764 worked upon it."[19]

The 1764 Covenant Chain Wampum was commissioned, and likely

designed, by Sir William Johnson and his wife-in-all-but-name Molly Brant (the extraordinary Haudenosaunee — Mohawk — clan mother) whose presentation signalled the Crown's understanding and ratification of the great Treaty in a way that acknowledged and respected Indigenous diplomacy. Likely woven by Indigenous women during the summer meetings, the chain evoked by this belt was one of silver, meaning that it required constant polishing in order to stay bright (reminding the various nations, including the British, that the relationship established at Niagara needed to be regularly communicated and renewed).

When Alan Corbiere read the Covenant Chain belt at Rama First Nation in 2013, he gifted the audience with a wonderful teaching given to him by Ken Maracle. Corbiere pointed to the seemingly unfinished diamonds at either end of the wampum, and told us that he asked Maracle why they would exist. Maracle then took the belt, joining the two ends together to create a circle — displaying how the wampum bridged both Indigenous (cyclical) and European (linear, presented by the date "1764") time. Since it

The *gustoweh* (headdress) of a Cayuga chief with antlers on display at the Woodland Cultural Centre in Brantford, Ontario. A headdress like this one is depicted on the chest of the Native figure on the Covenant Chain Wampum. *Courtesy of the Woodland Cultural Centre.*

The completed 1764 Covenant Chain Wampum replica held by Ken Maracle and the author. The replica was begun by Maracle on Manitoulin Island, and completed in the presence of the author on the territory of the Six Nations of the Grand River. *Courtesy of author*.

The Covenant Chain Wampum forming a circle, demonstrating Indigenous concepts of time and the cyclical nature of the seasons. *Courtesy of author*.

was commissioned by Sir William Johnson, the representative of the King, the Covenant Chain Wampum demonstrates that the Crown once understood and respected the different worldview of its partner.

The concept of a Covenant Chain is an ancient one, its origins stretching back to the very beginning of the relationship between early Dutch settlers and Indigenous populations on the northeastern coast of the continent in the early 1600s. The original description of the relationship was that the two peoples were linked together across a great distance by a rope. Attending a talk at Six Nations on the Grand River in 2014, I heard Jamie Jacobs (member of the Seneca Nation and collections assistant at the New York Rochester Museum and Science Centre) explain that the rope recalled those once used to tie the Dutch trading ships to the shore. As the Dutch traders moved further and further inland, the metaphorical rope was pulled deeper into Indigenous lands (eventually having one end fixed at the Onondaga Nation, in the heart of the Haudenosaunee Confederacy, and the other at Albany, the closest European trading centre).[20] The Dutch and Haudenosaunee eventually strengthened their relationship to the point that the rope was replaced by an iron chain. After a series of wars, the Dutch were replaced by the English and a new chain was forged, this one made of silver. Addressing a Haudenosaunee Council in 1755 Sir William Johnson detailed his understanding of the history of the Covenant Chain:

> That upon your first acquaintance we shook hands & finding we should be useful to another entered into a Covenant of Brothery Love & mutual Friendship. And tho' we were at first only ties [sic] together by a Rope, yet lest this rope grow rotten & break we ties ourselves together by an Iron Chain. Lest time or accident might rust & destroy this Chain of Iron, we afterwards made one of Silver, the strength and brightness of which would subject it to no decay. The ends of this Silver Chain we fix't to the Immovable Mountains, and this in so firm a manner that no Mortal enemy

might be able to remove it.... You know also that this Covenant Chain of Love and Friendship was the Dread & Envy of all your Enemies & ours, that by keeping it bright & unbroken we have never spilt in anger one drop of each other's blood to this day.

Emphasizing that the Covenant Chain constituted a relationship that required constant attention and renewal, Johnson went on to say:

You well know also that from the beginning to this time we have almost every year, strengthened & brightened this Covenant Chain in the most public & solemn manner. You know that we come as one body, one blood & one people ... I am now ready with this belt [*described as "the Union Belt"*] in the Great King your Father's name, to renew, to make more strong & bright than

The Friendship Wampum displayed during the commemorations of the 250th anniversary of the Treaty of Niagara held near Niagara-on-the-Lake August 2, 2014. This belt depicts an early representation of the Covenant Chain relationship, shown as a rope tying the Native man (right) to the Dutch (left) in the sixteenth and seventeenth centuries. *Courtesy of author.*

ever, the Covenant Chain of Love and Friendship between all the English upon this Continent & you're the Confederate Nations here present, all your Allies and dependents and that it now be agreed between us, that those who are Friends or Enemies to the English shall be considered such by the Confederate Nations their Allies & Dependents, & that your Friends and Enemies shall be ours.[21]

The Covenant Chain was a complex relationship that provided a forum to resolve disputes and make formal grievances, and extended beyond the Haudenosaunee and Western Nations. By 1725, the Mi'kmaq and Maliseet representatives were in Boston concluding the first of many Peace and Friendship Treaties, establishing their own Covenant Chain relationships throughout the eastern shores of North America. These systems of conflict resolution based on mutual respect and familial love are key frameworks that must be rediscovered by Canadians.

In his book *An Ethic of Mutual Respect: The Covenant Chain and Aboriginal-Crown Relations*, Bruce Morito reminds his reader that the Covenant Chain relationship was a practical one, facilitating the needs of those nations bound to it. Morito cautions that the Covenant Chain should neither be idealized nor overly defined. He emphasizes that the Covenant Chain was not forged during a "golden age of Crown-Aboriginal relations," rather that it was established in an environment of "war, intrigue, hard-edged and often illicit trading practices, and an array of related conflicts."[22] These were real relationships with all the complexity and subtle nuances that came with them. Just as the closest of Nations, or the most trusted and loved family members, can come to bitter disagreement, so too could those bound together by the Covenant Chain. Such a binding of equals would necessitate regular gatherings and councils — "getting everyone on the same page" as Alan Corbiere once explained — to polish the Silver Chain. Emphasizing the loving relationship that treaties encompass, meetings would often begin with the exchange of condolence strings of wampum to recognize loss of members in their respective communities.[23]

Receiving the 1764 Covenant Chain Wampum, the Odawa were entrusted with its care.[24] It was said during the ceremony that the wampum would be kept at Michilimackinac,[25] "as it is the Centre, where all our People may see it."[26] The Odawa remain the keepers of this wampum, although the original presented at Niagara has been lost.

A second belt, the Twenty-Four Nations Wampum, was also commissioned and presented by Johnson to the assembled Nations that day, signalling that they were now linked through each other to the British Crown. If ever one of the Nations were in need of protection or support, or if there were a problem in the relationship, all they needed to do was shake the belt (sending a message down through the other nations to the British) in order for the Crown to respond.

Grand Council Chief Patrick Madahbee and Rick Hill display the Twenty-Four Nations Wampum to the crowd gathered at Fort Niagara to commemorate the 250th anniversary of the Treaty of Niagara. The lieutenant governor of Ontario sits in the front row as Alan Corbiere explains the wampum's significance. *Courtesy of author.*

THE 1764 TREATY OF NIAGARA AND COVENANT CHAIN OF FRIENDSHIP

Johnson also presented twenty-four medals to the Nations present at Niagara. Embossed with the date "1764," the medals are described by Alan Corbiere as featuring "... a British Man and an Anishinaabe sitting under a tree, smoking, while a fire smoulders in the background." Corbiere points out that the medal features a depiction of a mat, symbolizing "... land, territory and peaceful relations." Corbiere comments that, while the 1764 Covenant Chain Wampum does not depict a mat, the image was evoked in the accompanying talk during the council at Niagara. [27]

In response to these gifts, the Western Nations presented Johnson with the *Teioháte Kaswenta* (Two Paths/Roads Wampum in the Mohawk language[28]), affirming that their understanding of the Treaty continued the Haudenosuanee vision of two peoples sharing the land as separate but equal partners. The *Teioháte Kaswenta* is an ancient agreement first entered into by the Haudenosuanee and Dutch traders in the seventeenth century and is explained by the Onondaga Nation as follows:

Obverse (depicting King George III) and reverse of the medal presented by Sir William Johnson to the Western Nations at the conclusion of the negotiations resulting in the signing of the Treaty of Niagara. *Library and Archives Canada, Acc. No. 1986-79-1612.*

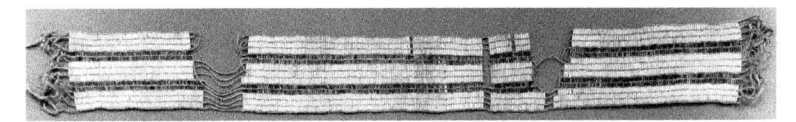

Image of an original, damaged *Teiohàte Kaswenta* (Two-Row Wampum belt), repatriated by the Heye Foundation (Museum of the American Indian at the Smithsonian Institution). *Courtesy of the Woodland Cultural Centre.*

> The Haudenosuanee told the Dutch that we do not use paper to record our history. We use … belts made of white and purple wampum shells. That we have made a belt to record this agreement. The belt is two purple rows running alongside each other representing two boats. In one, is the canoe with our way of life, laws and people. In the other is your ship with your laws, religion, and people in it. Our boats will travel side by side down the river of life. That each will respect the ways of each other and will not interfere with the other.[29]

Writing about the Treaty of Niagara in the *Toronto Star* on July 1, 2014, Ryerson Professor Hayden King challenged the idea of "Canada Day" as the celebration of the birth of the country. For King, the conclusion of the Treaty of Niagara is a more authentic birthdate for the country, highlighting its unfulfilled potential.

"The treaty [of Niagara]," Hayden wrote, "permitted the sharing of the land across the eastern continent and mutual recognition of autonomy among distinct people rooted in peace, friendship and respect. Without it there would be no Canada, neither in ideational nor material terms."[30]

For decades after their presentation by Johnson the Covenant Chain and Twenty-Four Nations Wampum were kept at Michilimackinac before being moved, along with the annual meeting to exchange gifts with the Crown, to Manitoulin Island in 1836. During the Manitoulin Island Treaty of 1836, Lieutenant Governor Sir Francis Bond Head directly referenced the council at Niagara, as well as the relationship it established with the King (now King William IV):

Seventy snow seasons have now passed away since we met in council at the crooked place (Niagara) at which time your Great Father, the King and the Indians of North America tied their hands together by the Wampum of friendship.[31]

That the lieutenant governor was emphasizing that the peoples at Manitoulin Island were bound to the King (implying equal standing with him) is important. Seventy years earlier, Sir William Johnson understood that First Nations never saw themselves as subjects of King George III, nor were they surrendering control, or sovereignty over their lands to the Crown. Two months after the Treaty of Niagara was established, Johnson wrote to Commander-in-Chief General Thomas Gage after hearing reports that Colonel John Bradstreet had dispatched someone to the Western Nations to have them swear an oath to King George III as subjects:[32]

> … I know it has been verry customary for many People to Insinuate that the Indians call themselves Subjects, altho I am thoroughly convinced they were never so called, nor would they approve of it … you may be assured that none of the Six Nations, Western Indians &ca. ever declared themselves to be subjects, or ever will consider themselves in that light whilst they have any Men or open Country to retire to, the very Idea of Subjection would fill them with horror.[33]

Indeed, Sir William Johnson reminded Colonel Henry Bouquet in 1764 that the Western Nations had no equivalent words for *subjection* and *dominion*.[34] In fact, rather than seeing themselves as subjects of the King, First Nations saw themselves in a personal partnership with an equal.

In a telephone conversation, the Honourable Steven L. Point, twenty-eighth lieutenant governor of British Columbia (the first Indigenous person to fill that high office in the province), explained that local colonial governments could not be trusted in a Treaty relationship because of their thirst for land. This is why Treaty was always made with the Monarch directly and not his or her subjects — the Treaty relationship is a very personal one with the individual wearing the Crown. In the twenty-first century, Treaty remains with the Queen herself, and not with her governments in Canada or the United Kingdom.[35]

Such sentiments are echoed throughout contemporary expressions of the Treaty relationship by Indigenous peoples, including the First Nations University of Canada, which published the following statement for the 2012 visit of the Prince of Wales and Duchess of Cornwall:

> One of the most important symbols in modern First Nations culture is our relationship with the British Crown. The concept of the Crown is one that embodies the entire nation of British colonial settlers. It is a bridge between the past and the future of those people who make up the country we now call Canada. It is this timeless quality that makes our relationship to the Crown important. We did not sign our Treaties with a particular government or political party. Governments come and go; public opinion waxes and wanes. Our bond was forged with the entire British and Canadian nations, past, present and future, as embodied by the monarchy.

Indeed, when the Queen visited the university in 2005 she presented a stone from Balmoral Castle to the institution as a tangible link between it and the Crown explaining:

> This stone was taken from the grounds of Balmoral Castle in the Highlands of Scotland — a place dear to my great-great-grandmother, Queen Victoria. It symbolises the foundation of the rights of First Nations peoples reflected in treaties signed

with the Crown during her reign. Bearing the cypher of Queen Victoria as well as my own, this stone is presented to the First Nations University of Canada in the hope that it will serve as a reminder of the special relationship between the Sovereign and all First Nations peoples.[36]

Such modern expressions of Treaty relationships reflect that, whether or not the colonial and Canadian officials of the past understood the obligations they were placing on the Monarch when they drafted the text of their Treaty documents, they certainly created them through their diplomatic prose.

The relationship outlined in the Royal Proclamation of 1763 has informed all Treaties between the Crown and First Nations since, including the "Numbered Treaties" that spread west from Upper Canada (Ontario). George III's words became the metre-stick against which everything since has been measured, making the Royal Proclamation relevant to Indigenous peoples from coast to coast to coast.

Even provinces such as British Columbia and Quebec, noted for their lack of treaties, reference the Royal Proclamation when engaging in modern negotiations. For years the validity of the Royal Proclamation in British Columbia was hotly contested, until 1984 when the Supreme Court of Canada ruled in *Guerin v. The Queen* that Indigenous title existed independently from the Proclamation. The government of Premier Gordon Campbell even considered drafting a new Royal Proclamation in 2009 (to be proclaimed by Lieutenant Governor Steven Point) which would supplement and complement the old one.[37]

In the third chapter of his forthcoming book, *Understanding Canada: A Country Based on Incomplete Conquests*, noted political scientist and author Dr. Peter Russell echoes Hayden King, declaring the Treaty of Niagara as Canada's "First Confederation."[38] Dr. John Borrows writes in "Wampum at Niagara: The Royal Proclamation, Canadian Legal History, and Self-Government":

The Queen presents a stone tablet from the grounds of her beloved Balmoral Castle (a place of significance for both her and her great-great grandmother Queen Victoria) to the First Nations University of Canada in 2005. *Courtesy of the Government of Saskatchewan.*

... the Royal Proclamation of 1763 is not only a "fundamental document" but, along with the Treaty of Niagara, the most "fundamental agreement" yet entered into between First Nations and the Crown, and much more than a unilateral declaration of the Crown's will.[39]

However, a key part of this relationship is being ignored by Canada. Commemorating the 250th anniversary of King George's Royal Proclamation the federal Ministry of Aboriginal Affairs and Northern Development published an explanation of the document for the general public. One of its posters declared:

Since its issuance in 1763, the Royal Proclamation has served as the basis of the treaty-making process throughout Canada. The protocols and procedures it established led to the orderly opening of the lands for settlement and the establishment of an ongoing Treaty Relationship between First Nations and the Crown. It also led to the establishment of the Indian Department's primary role as intermediary between First Nation peoples and the Crown. After Confederation in 1867, the principles established by the Proclamation continued to guide the treaties of Western Canada and the establishment of treaty rights and obligations for all parties.[40]

The Treaty of Niagara, including the terms (recited and recorded in wampum) and the relationship it created, are not mentioned by the ministry. Similarly, while Governor General David Johnston participated in a symposium hosted by the Land Claims Agreement Coalition honouring the Royal Proclamation on October 7, 2013, nothing was done the following year to acknowledge the council at Niagara (even though His Excellency had mentioned the Treaty in previous speeches made years earlier).

Speaking at the 2013 symposium, the governor general remarked that "The Royal Proclamation showed the way forward for the country that would become Canada" and that it "laid the basis for the recognition of First Nations rights, and defined the relationship between First Nations peoples and the Crown."[41] However, if only the written document is acknowledged, and not the equally important oral commitments sealed in wampum, the relationship remains empty.

If the ideals of Canada captured in such documents as the 1960 Canadian Bill of Rights, and later the 1982 Canadian Charter of Rights and Freedoms, are to be realized, the Treaty of Niagara and the Silver Covenant Chain, which serve to bind First Nations to the Queen (and therefore Canada), must also be placed at the heart of our democracy. The mention of the 1982 Canadian Charter of Rights and Freedoms, part of Canada's Constitution, is deliberate, since Section 25 acknowledges that the government must honour the treaties, citing the Royal Proclamation:

> 25. The guarantee in this Charter of certain rights and freedoms shall not be construed so as to abrogate or derogate from any aboriginal, treaty or other rights or freedoms that pertain to the aboriginal peoples of Canada including:
>
> a) any rights or freedoms that have been recognized by the Royal Proclamation of October 7, 1763; and
>
> b) any rights or freedoms that now exist by way of land claims agreements or may be so acquired.[42]

The Charter pulls the Royal Proclamation into modern Canada, making its fulfillment by Canadians not just morally and ethically necessary, but also a constitutional directive. However, King George's

Proclamation must be seen alongside the Treaty of Niagara in order for it to become authentic. Without including what was sealed by wampum in 1764, an incomplete picture of the relationship, which includes a singular link with the Queen, between Canada and First Nations will persist. The consequences of an unrealized relationship and ignored Treaties speak for themselves.

Within a few short decades of the council at Niagara, a colonial government was established that would turn so dramatically against First Nations that the father of my friend, Eugene Kahgee, made a pact in the 1960s with his best friend that saw them whipped every day they were held at the Mohawk Institute Residential School just to remind themselves that they were still "Indians." A feature of our democracy, rule by majority, opened the doors to increasingly devastating policies imposed by the colonial, and later Canadian, governments following the War of 1812 (the last instance where First Nations allies were essential to the preservation of British North America). Constitutionally separated from the Dignified Crown, the elected governments of the nineteenth and twentieth centuries pursued policies of assimilation that included the 1876 Indian Act as well as the Indian Residential School System that flowed from it. Since Confederation, elected officials in Canada have ignored the Covenant Chain, forbidding the Queen (or King) from taking a seat at the council fires.

A fascinating letter was published by Peter Carstens in 1991 illustrating how far the relationship had deteriorated, and how the Government of Canada had inserted itself into the personal relationship between the Queen and Aboriginal peoples. Carstens explained how his Okanagan friend had written to the Queen in 1982 to detail "Canada's violation of various informal agreements over land that were reached with Chief Nkwala in the mid-nineteenth century." The Queen never received the letter; instead, Carstens's friend was sent an unsigned response from the Department of Indian and Northern Affairs. Apparently, once the letter arrived at Buckingham Palace, it was immediately forwarded to the governor general of Canada, whose office passed it to the minister of Indian Affairs.

Carstens's friend then sent another letter, this time to the Department of Indian and Northern Affairs, demanding to know by whose authority his letter to the Queen had been intercepted. The signed response by Minister John Munro captures succinctly the approach of the Government of Canada to the Treaty relationship:

> The authority of The Queen to deal with matters concerning Indians in Canada has lawfully been passed by Her and by the Parliament of the United Kingdom to the Parliament and Government of Canada. The Parliament of Canada, acting under these legal powers, has in turn enacted the *Indian Act* which entrusts to me, as Minister of Indian Affairs, the responsibility of administering that Act. It was for this reason that your letter … was referred to me from the Governor General's Office.… The legality of this transfer of authority over Indian Affairs matters in Canada was upheld by the English Court of Appeal and by the House of Lords during the winter of 1981–1982. It was therefore not only legally proper for your letter to be sent to me, but I, with the assistance of my officers, am the only person to whom it could properly be sent.

"Well Pete, I guess that's it," Carstens's friend remarked "That Ottawa *tyhee* [big shot] has got all the power now, and the Queen and I have none."[43]

CHAPTER THREE

# The Queen at the Council Fire

First Nations correctly see that sovereignty in this country is vested in the Crown. However, cemented into Canada's constitutional monarchy is the convention of responsible government, which requires that the Sovereign and her representatives (the Dignified Crown) be advised by elected ministers (the Efficient Crown) before acting on nearly every issue. This means that, for non-Indigenous Canadians, the Crown articulated in the 1700s and early 1800s no longer exists (and arguably never truly existed at all). Many Indigenous peoples do not accept this premise and see their relationship as being with Elizabeth II in her role as the British Monarch, regarding the Canadian Crown (a political reality for non-Indigenous Canadians since the 1931 Statute of Westminster) as an interloper. Oftentimes, the link with Queen Elizabeth II and the Royal Family is articulated in terms of their lineage to King George III or Queen Victoria (the monarchs in whose names treaties were often concluded). Elizabeth II is important because she is the great-great-granddaughter of Queen Victoria.

Peter Russell addressed this disconnect between Indigenous and non-Indigenous Canadian perspectives concerning the Crown when he wrote:

… Canada has become a self-governing democracy. Some might say this means that Aboriginal people should adjust to this reality and give up counting on an honourable crown as their partner in regulating their relationship with Canada. But why should they do that? They were never consulted about these huge changes in the nature of their treaty partner. They were totally excluded from participation of any kind in the discussions and negotiations that led to Confederation and the founding of the Dominion of Canada.[1]

The Honourable Steven Point was more direct when we spoke over the phone. "Nobody told the Indians!" he said when asked about the changes to the Crown/First Nations relationship created during the 1982 Canada Act negotiations (the most recent additions to the country's written constitution).

During her 2012–2013 hunger strike,[2] Attawapiskat chief Theresa Spence, infused with the frustration and energy of the Idle No More movement, corresponded with Governor General David Johnston following a reception held at Rideau Hall on January 11, 2013. In her letter, Spence laid out what she saw as the responsibilities of the governor general:

> I write this letter to stress the importance of the position that you hold in relation to the original treaties made with First Nations and the Crown and it is imperative that yourself and the Prime Minister be present at a meeting of all First Nation Chiefs to discuss concerns and renew the relationship with First Nations in Canada.[3]

Having the governor general in the same room with the prime minister during a policy discussion with First Nations blurs the lines of responsible government, however, as the Dignified Crown is no longer a politically active player.

Johnston responded to Spence's letter with a reminder of the political constraints he faced. "As you may be aware, in our system of constitutional monarchy," His Excellency wrote, "the governor general acts on the advice of Canadian ministers; the matters you raise are their direct responsibility...."[4]

The governor general's gentle reminder of the convention of responsible government was immediately rejected by Chief Spence, who, three days later, replied:

> Your office maintains and exercises a direct role and duty in respect to addressing these concerns. It continues to fall on your office to uphold the Honor of the Crown and to provide your opinion and advice to the Prime Minister and to Her Majesty's Privy Council. It remains the duty of your office, as Her Majesty's representative in Canada, to maintain watch and to ensure the faithful performance of the terms of the Treaty entered into between the Crown and the First Nations in Canada.

In a direct demand for the Dignified Crown to become an active agent in the relationship between Canada and First Nations, Spence continued:

> In accordance with the [C]onstitution and with the *Letters Patent Constituting the Office of Governor General and Commander in Chief of Canada*, your office also holds certain reserve powers which may be invoked where it is your opinion there in an intolerable violation of the spirit and intent of the constitution over an extended period of time, and where there is doubt as to the righteousness and constitutionality of the actions of your office. Moreover, Your Excellency must advert to assertions of intolerable violations of the spirit and intent of the constitution and respond to such assertions.[5]

When one looks at the "post-responsible government" Dignified Crown through the lens of treaties that are considered as living familial relationships, the sense of betrayal for Indigenous peoples is understandable. Few non-Indigenous Canadians expect, nor would tolerate, the idea of Queen Elizabeth II personally involving herself in the day-to-day running of the country (influencing and modifying government policy, legislation, etc.). Yet, one year after her correspondence with the governor general, Chief Spence wrote an open letter to the national chief of the Assembly of First Nations, the Nishnawbe Aski Nation grand chief, and the Ontario regional chief declaring:

> Modern developments by various Provincial, and Federal governments have eroded this historical relationship [between the Crown and First Nations], with the tacit approval, or ignorance of Her Majesty the Queen, who had promised to protect her people.[6]

Spence's critique of the Queen is deeply personal. The Covenant Chain binding the Crown and First Nations is described as not only dulled, but eroded. The Sovereign is portrayed as someone who has either actively, or through her own inaction, participated in the destruction of *her* people.

Examples of similar sentiments can be found across Canada, including a 2013 open letter by Ontario Regional Chief Stan Beardy to the Queen asking Her Majesty to "directly intervene in the ongoing crisis in Canada in order to protect First Nations against the onslaught of the federal government," even suggesting she "… should consider visiting Canada and using [her] good offices to ensure that [her] government in Canada lives up to the spirit and intent of the Royal Proclamation of 1763."[7]

When asked at the end of the Indigenous Bar Association's 2013 annual general meeting what he thought needed to happen concerning Canada's treatment of First Nations, Justice Murray Sinclair responded, "We need to go see the Queen. [Six hundred and fifty] chiefs standing outside Buckingham Palace telling her that her government in this country does not uphold the honour of the Crown."[8]

Sinclair's suggestion echoes one made earlier that year by delegates at the Assembly of First Nations National Treaty Forum (March 26–27), and highlighted by National Chief Shawn A-in-chut Atleo in *Nation to Nation: A Resource on Treaties in Ontario*, which asked for a strategy to be developed that would result in an audience with "Her Royal Majesty, the Queen of England in this the 250th anniversary of the Royal Proclamation."[9]

If Canada is to restore the relationship represented by both the *Teioháte Kaswenta* and the 1764 Covenant Chain Wampum, the Indigenous perspective of the Crown must be addressed. Even within the strictures of responsible government, the Dignified Crown can still act in a way that Indigenous peoples' concerns and demands can be addressed and validated. This is especially true when concerning the powers of the Dignified Crown that remain, called "rights" in Walter Bagehot's seminal *The English Constitution*, a source often cited by lieutenant governors and governors general when explaining their positions to the public:

The right to be consulted;
The right to encourage;
The right to warn.[10]

If these rights have indeed been transmitted to the Canadian Crown (their exercise usually depends on the strength of the vice-regal office, or the already existing relationship between the Queen's representative and his (or her) respective first minister) an important conduit remains to advocate for, or facilitate communication with, First Nations. Addressing a gathering after his induction as an honorary witness to the Truth and Reconciliation Commission, Lieutenant Governor David Onley remarked that the relationship between the Crown and

First Nations is unique. As the official representative of the Queen in Ontario, Onley explained that the lieutenant governor has a role that no government or bureaucracy could fill. Reflecting on the modern role of the Queen's representative, Onley raised the historic continuity of the Canadian Crown and its relationships with First Nations for "as long as the sun shines, the grass grows and the rivers flow." Onley went on to conclude, "This means there is an historic, legal, and ethical obligation between the Vice Regal Office and Ontario's Aboriginal Peoples."[11]

What cements the Monarch in the very heart of the Treaty relationship is that, from the very beginning of the British Crown's interaction with First Nations, the Monarch, as an individual, has always been presented as having personally invested in the relationship. A long history of personal interactions between Indigenous peoples and the Monarch, the Royal Family, and the Monarch's official representatives attests to this relationship.

During the first Royal Tour of Upper Canada in 1792, a delegation representing various First Nations met with King George III's son, Prince Edward Augustus, on the same spot where the Covenant Chain Wampum had been exchanged thirty years previous. During his interview with the delegation, Prince Edward (the future father of Queen Victoria) was given the name "Chief-Above-All-Other-Chiefs." All in all, the meeting had a strong impact on the King's son. Writing back to his father, Edward's observations reflect that a deeply personal relationship had been reaffirmed by First Nations on the shores of the Niagara River:

> A very large deputation from the Indians of all neighbouring nations came to Niagara to wait my arrival, as soon as they heard I was to visit Upper Canada. Their professions of attachment to Your Majesty and the British Government were extremely warm, and they would not on any account return home to their tribes till they made me faithfully promise that in the name of them all I should inform you, in the strongest words I could find, of

their zealous *attachment to your person* [author's emphasis], and of their utmost readiness at all times to obey any commands with which you may at any time chuse [*sic*] to honour them.[12]

Sixty years later, the historic Royal Tour of Canada by the Prince of Wales (the future King Edward VII) encompassed many meetings with First Nations. During preparations for the tour, Henry Pelham (the fifth Duke of Newcastle and secretary of state for war and the colonies) had officially been instructed by Queen Victoria to "… enquire into the condition of her Indian subjects in this country, whose complaints have recently reached the Royal Ear."

Earlier that year, the Queen had been visited by the Mississauga/Anishinaabe Nahnebahwequay (Catherine Sutton), who informed Her Majesty of the ill treatment of her people by the Indian Department in

Portrait of Kahkewaquonaby (Reverend Peter Jones) made by David Octavius Hill and Robert Adamson in 1845. *Library and Archives Canada, R11326-0-9-E.*

Canada. Nahnebahwequay's meeting with Queen Victoria was noted in the Royal diary, with the Anishinaabe recording in her own journal that the Queen had asked her many questions and promised aid and protection for her people.[13]

Nahnebahwequay's audience with Queen Victoria was nothing new. In fact, she was following in the footsteps of many Anishinaabe leaders including her uncle Kahkewaquonaby (Reverend Peter Jones). Kahkewaquonaby, a famous Mississauga of the New Credit chief and a Wesleyan minister, spent his life advocating for his people to have their ownership of lands along the Credit River recognized by the Crown. Tirelessly lobbying the representatives of the Crown in Canada, Kahkewaquonaby also travelled extensively in the United Kingdom (often speaking to members of the Wesleyan church). Highlighting the personal relationship between the Monarch and First Nations, Kahkewaquonaby visited King William and Queen Adelaide along with a Mi'kmaq chief and his son in 1832. The audience with the King and Queen lasted thirty minutes and included a presentation to William IV of an Anishinaabe translation of the Gospel of St. John by Kahkewaquonaby himself. Conversation was kept light and focused mainly on the dress of Their Majesty's Anishinaabe and Mi'kmaq guests.[14]

Kahkewaquonaby's September 14, 1838, visit to Queen Victoria was much more focused, and thoroughly documented in his diary:

> ... I bowed two or three times as I approached the Queen, which she returned, approaching me at the same time, and holding out her hand as a signal for me to kiss. I went down upon my right knee, and holding out my arm, she put her hand upon the back of my hand, which I pressed to my lips and kissed. I then said that I had great pleasure in laying before Her Majesty a petition from the Indians residing at the River Credit in Upper Canada, which that people had sent by me; that I was happy to say Lord Glenelg [secretary of state for war and the colonies] (pointing to his Lordship,)

had already granted the prayer of the petition, by requesting the Governor of Upper Canada, to give the Indians the title-deeds they asked for. His Lordship bowed to Her Majesty, and she bowed in token of approbation of His Lordship's having granted the thing prayed for by her red children; that I presented the petition to Her Majesty, thinking she would like to possess such a document as a curiosity, as the Wampum attached to it had a meaning, and their totams marked opposite the names of the Indians who signed it. The Queen then said, "I thank you, sir, I am much obliged to you." I then proceeded to give her the meaning of the Wampum; and told her that the white Wampum signified the loyal and good feeling which prevails amongst the Indians towards Her Majesty and Her Government; but that the black Wampum was designed to tell Her Majesty that their hearts were troubled on account of their having no title-deeds for their lands; and that they had sent their petition and Wampum that Her Majesty might be pleased to take out all the black Wampum, so that the string might all be white....[15]

Miniature watercolour portrait of Queen Victoria, ca. 1840. Artist unknown. Library and Archives Canada, Acc. No. 1959-1-6.

Everything about this meeting highlights a relationship of respect and affirmation, and was even noted by the Queen in her personal diary.[16] The presentation of the petition to the Queen honoured her Treaty relationship with the Mississaugas/Anishinaabe, reinforcing it as a familial one. While responsible government dictated that it was the decision of the colonial secretary to grant the title-deeds, the Covenant Chain required the personal involvement of the Monarch in physically receiving the petition and assenting to it. The Queen's participation made this a meeting of kin — a moment that went beyond simply a political act (which only the government could perform) to become part of a larger, personal relationship (or Covenant) between the Dignified Crown and Indigenous peoples. The continued use of wampum as a medium of communication and memory should be noted.

Over 175 years later, when the Mississaugas of the New Credit were invited into the Ontario Legislature for the first time to sing a welcoming song for Premier Kathleen Wynne's newly sworn-in Executive Council, Elder Garry Sault began by presenting both the premier and Lieutenant Governor David Onley with strings of wampum touched by his council, saying, "This Wampum is a reminder that it's 250 years [since] the Treaty of Niagara.… So we visit you with this Wampum to stir the fires so that you can once again start to polish that great Covenant Chain."[17]

Sadly, the results of Newcastle's observations made during the 1860 Royal Tour were hindered by the evolution of constitutional monarchy in British North America. Due to responsible government, Queen Victoria had to follow the advice of her elected ministers concerning the government's actions with First Nations. Due to the passage of John A. Macdonald's Management of Indian Lands and Property Act (Indian Land Act) on June 30, 1860, the commissioner of Crown lands in the Province of Canada also became the superintendent of Indian Affairs, transferring "Indian Affairs" from the Imperial government in London to the colonial authorities. The Duke of Newcastle's inquiry now fell under the direction of Richard Pennefather, the governor general's civil secretary and superintendent-general of Indian Affairs in the Province of Canada.[18] Pennefather wrote an eighty-two-page report defending the Indian Department, which Newcastle accepted, presenting it to the Queen with his own notation: "I hope that the Advocates of the Indians in this Country who have frequently called on you and have written … are now persuaded that there really is not much to complain of in Canada."[19]

A watercolour of Edward, Prince of Wales, painted around the time of his 1860 Royal Tour of Canada by William Lockwood (1803–1866). *Library and Archives Canada, MIKAN no. 3636417.*

Nahnebahwequay was furious with the duke, arguing (correctly) that his investigation had been done through the lens of the negligent department. Constitutionally bound, the Queen accepted the report.

The Haudenosaunee also personally appealed to the Prince of Wales during his visit to Brantford, Ontario, in 1860, even though he made no note of it in his regular letters to his mother. Quoted by J.R. (Jim) Miller in his essay "The Aboriginal Peoples and the Canadian Crown," the address by the nineteen-year-old Oronhyatekha (Peter Martin) referred to the Prince of Wales as an equal (i.e., "brother") and invoked both the Great Spirit and Covenant Chain:

> Brother, — We, the Chiefs, Sachems, and Warriors of the Six Nations in Canada are glad of the opportunity to welcome to our native land the Son of our Gracious Sovereign Queen Victoria, and to manifest our continued loyalty and devotion to the person and Crown of your Royal Mother. We return thanks to the Great Spirit that has put into your Royal Highness's mind to come to

this country, and that He has preserved your Royal Highness safe, that we may meet together this day. He has ordained Princes and Rulers to govern his people; and it is His will that our beloved Queen, Your Royal Mother, is so preeminent in power and virtue.

Brother, — Although we have been separated from our Sovereign by the "Great Water," yet have we ever kept *the chain of friendship bright, and it gives us joy to meet with the Heir Apparent to the Throne, that we may renew and strengthen that chain, which has existed between the Crown of England and the Six Nations for more than two hundred years* [author's emphasis]. Our confidence in our Sovereign is as lasting as the stars in Heaven. We rejoice at the presence among us to fill the place of your Royal Mother, and her illustrious predecessor, whom we also love."[20]

Oronhyatekha, a brilliant young man with a photographic memory, became a lifelong friend of the Prince of Wales's attending physician, Sir Henry Acland. It was Prince Edward that suggested Oronhyatekha attend university at Oxford in England, beginning a remarkable connection between the Mohawk and the Royal Family. In the course of his extraordinary life, Oronhyatekha graduated from the University of Toronto with a medical degree, became a regular visitor to the Court of Queen Victoria (even obtaining Royal permission to replicate the coronation chair for his own collection), and was appointed supreme chief ranger of the Independent Order of Foresters. Dr. Oronhyatekha rode with Governor General the Earl of Aberdeen in 1895 when the viceroy came to Toronto to lay the cornerstone of the Temple Building, and attended the coronation of his patron, now King Edward VII, in 1902.[21]

Such presentations and interactions can be found throughout Canada's Royal Tours, and remain features today. During the 2014 Royal Tour of Manitoba, Grand Chief Derek Nepinak openly discussed treaties with the Prince of Wales, including the near-unanimous condemnation of the much hated Bill C-33 (First Nations Control of First Nations

A sketch of Oronhyatekha made by Sir Henry Acland during the 1860 Royal visit to Six Nations by the Prince of Wales. *Library and Archives Canada, Acc. No. 1986-7-255.*

Chief Beardy presents gifts to the Princess Royal during a meeting in the Vice-Regal Suite of Queen's Park, Toronto. October 23, 2013. *Courtesy of the Office of the Lieutenant Governor of Ontario.*

Education Act). Quoted in a CBC article discussing Nepinak's actions, Niigaanwewidam James Sinclair, an assistant professor in Native studies at the University of Manitoba, explained, "[Prince Charles] has a great deal of sway and control and influence with the federal government through the Governor General."[22]

Such statements make many political scientists nervous across this country, but it must be understood that they reflect a long-standing tradition that should not be ignored or taken lightly.

Petitions and grievances presented by First Nations leaders to the Sovereign and members of the Royal Family increased dramatically during the 1970s. Meeting the Queen in Manitoba during a ceremony in 1970, David Courchene (head of the Manitoba Indian Brotherhood) urged her to "… advocate on our behalf to your loyal ministers" for better understanding and Indigenous participation in the decision making process. [23]

Three years later, Queen Elizabeth responded in Alberta with a statement prepared by both the federal government and the Indian Association of Alberta (this statement would be quoted by National Chief Shawn Atleo during the 2012 Crown/First Nations Gathering in Ottawa):

> You may be confident of the continued cooperation of my government which represents your people as it represents all the people of Canada. You may be assured that my government of Canada recognizes the importance of full compliance with the spirit and terms of your treaties.
>
> I am deeply impressed with the pride of heritage which has sustained you through so many dramatic changes and difficulties. I hope this very sense of identity will help find on your own a truly Indian place in the modern world.[24]

That these words were spoken by the Queen are significant. That they were written in consultation with Indigenous peoples is key. While acknowledging the realities of responsible government, the Crown is still able to evoke the personal relationship required to maintain the Covenant Chain. In the context of the Canadian Constitution, the Queen's words are those of the State, and that the Indian Association of Alberta had a role in sculpting them is an important watershed in the relationship.

A remarkable dispatch exists marked CONFIDENTIAL and LOCSEN[25] by Sir Peter Hayman (British high commissioner in Canada, 1970–1974) to Sir Alec Douglas-Home (foreign secretary, 1970–1974) assessing the general question of the monarchy in Canada following the Queen's two Royal Tours of the country (June 25 to July 5, and July 31 to August 4, 1973). Forwarded to Buckingham Palace (under cover as a personal and confidential letter to Sir Martin Charteris, assistant private secretary to the Queen), the dispatch highlighted the British government's discussion around the separation between the Canadian and British monarchies, and the Queen's role in both offices.

Describing the delicacy of Hayman's notes, H.T.A. Overton of the Foreign and Commonwealth Office's North America Department responded to Sir Peter, saying, "The basic difficulty of handling rests upon the difficulty, which you rightly illuminated, of distinguishing between Her Majesty's British and Canadian capacities, in the practical as well as in the formal sense."[26]

Titled "The Monarchy in Canada, 1973," Hayman's dispatch described the June 25 – July 5 tour as "the most political" visit that any monarch had paid to Canada, and included an extraordinary passage referencing the Queen's historic address in Calgary, Alberta:

> On a more serious political issue, The Queen's speeches to the Indians in the West were undoubted contributions to the handling of this intractable problem. As Canada develops her North — potentially so rich in natural resources — the problem of native rights will become increasingly serious. Two of the Canadians most deeply involved in these problems [unnamed in the dispatch, but one is likely Jean Chrétien[27]] have told me that the existence of the Monarchy and the fact that, on occasions, The Queen can talk directly to the native peoples has helped to prevent in Canada anything like a direct confrontation similar to "Wounded Knee."[28]

In light of the personal connection of the Queen with Indigenous peoples, the Dignified Crown in Canada provides a unique opportunity to fuse the two Treaty partners into one person. The Honourable James K. Bartleman, twenty-seventh lieutenant governor of Ontario and member of the Chippewas of Mnjikaning First Nation, acknowledged this during a visit to his home territory on September 12, 2002:

It seems history has come full circle. More than two hundred years ago, the Anishinaabe people welcomed the First Lieutenant Governor of Upper Canada, ... John Graves Simcoe, to their territory. And now I, their descendant, am being welcomed by you as the Sovereign's representative ... [29]

While the country still waits for an Indigenous minister of aboriginal affairs and northern development to be appointed, the Queen of Canada's first official representative from the Indigenous community appeared in 1974 with the appointment as Alberta's lieutenant governor of Ralph Garvin Steinhauer of the Saddle Lake Cree Nation.[30] Steinhauer's appointment was another watershed moment for both the Dignified Crown and the Covenant Chain relationship. "It is a very large step I'm taking for the Native people," Steinhauer commented after being sworn into office.

Federal Justice Minister Otto Lang explained the importance of the event to the *Edmonton Journal* by saying, "The Queen's appointment of an Indian is historic in that it was a Queen [Victoria] who built a trust with the Indians of Canada so many years ago."[31]

A survivor of Brandon Indian Residential School, a former Liberal candidate (the first Indigenous candidate in a federal election), a member and then officer of the Order of Canada, and the elected chief of the Saddle Lake Cree Nation (1966–1969), Ralph Steinhauer immediately challenged constitutional conventions when he threatened to reactivate prerogatives that had long passed from the vice-regal office. In his 1976 speech delivered at the University of Calgary, Lieutenant Governor Steinhauer presented a list of injustices inflicted upon Indigenous peoples, even going so far as to suggest that he might withhold Royal Assent for legislation affecting First Nations until there was some improvement.[32]

That same year Steinhauer threatened to "depart from the traditional neutrality [of his office]," even going so far as to declare, "The Queen has the right to speak out. If I'm the representative of the Queen here, I have the same privilege."[33] (Under the convention of responsible government, the Queen does not have the right to speak out.)

This belief followed Lieutenant Governor Steinhauer as he headed a delegation commemorating the signing of Treaties Six and Seven to Buckingham Palace in July 1976. After being presented to the Queen, and disregarding orders from Ottawa to keep the meeting apolitical, the lieutenant governor proceeded to raise Indigenous issues with Her Majesty.

"You're going to get us in a lot of trouble you know," Prime Minister Pierre Trudeau once cautioned the lieutenant governor.

Steinhauer simply replied, "Is it that the truth hurts?"

"Possibly," the prime minister is said to have replied.[34]

A potential crisis nearly arose around the 1977 Land Title Amendment Act proposed by the provincial government, which would have blocked attempts by First Nations to declare their interests in the lands and resources of northern Alberta, including the Athabasca oil sands. Along with several First Nations, the Alberta Human Rights and Civil Liberties Association informed Lieutenant Governor Steinhauer of the Land Title Amendment Act's violation of Treaty rights and advised him to either refuse Royal Assent or resign his office. In the end, readily admitting that he had had the legislation studied by his legal firm, Steinhauer granted Royal Assent conceding, "I had no right to oppose it unless I could find that it is really contrary to the constitution in the makeup of the Bill."[35]

Steinhauer was the first to admit not understanding the constitutional role that vice-regal representative filled in the province, but he was a quick study. By the end of his term, the outgoing lieutenant governor reflected on the apolitical nature of his office in his various interviews with the media. In a 1979 interview with Jeff Sallott of the *Globe and Mail*, Steinhauer admitted to exercising his constitutional rights around consultation numerous times when he had opinions concerning provincial legislation. Becoming introspective, Steinhauer said, "I got my knuckles rapped for comments that might have been considered political. But," he added, "those were comments about past governments. I haven't commented on the current Government."[36]

While controversial, Ralph Steinhauer did engage Canadians with Indigenous peoples, reminding them of an important relationship (and responsibility). Before granting Royal Assent to legislation in the Alberta Legislature on July 4, 1979, Lieutenant Governor Steinhauer addressed the assembled members, reflecting on the fact that he was likely performing one his last duties in their company. Thanking the members for their good work in government, Steinhauer remarked, "May the Great Spirit remain with you, and will you always carry on such a well-done job."[37] It was the first time the Great Spirit had been invoked in the provincial legislature.

His most dramatic act of fusing both Treaty partners occurred when Steinhauer read the 1975 Speech from the Throne, representing the Queen of Canada, while dressed in the full regalia of a Nēhiraw chief. The image of Steinhauer enthroned is a powerful one, highlighting the

The Honourable Ralph Steinhauer reads the Speech from the Throne in his full Native regalia on January 23, 1975. *Courtesy of Provincial Archives of Alberta, 33167/3.*

complex history of this country and its relationship with Indigenous peoples. The 1975 opening of the Alberta Legislature was a seminal moment in the evolution of Canada's constitutional monarchy, something that had nothing to do with the contents of the Throne Speech. Truly, it was a moment when the Dignified Crown acted independently from its elected government to honour the Indigenous peoples of not only Alberta, but the land as a whole. Seeing Steinhauer in full regalia as the Queen's official representative emphasized the fact that, at least for his time in office, the relationship between the Queen and the Saddle Lake Cree Nation had been fused into one man, a unique aspect of Canada's dynamic constitutional monarchy.

The Honourable Ralph Steinhauer was only the first Indigenous appointment to a vice-regal office in this country. While there has yet to be an Indigenous governor general, Manitoba (the Honourable W. Yvon Dumont, 1993–1999), Ontario (the Honourable James K. Bartleman, 2002–2007), British Columbia (the Honourable Steven L. Point, 2007–2012), and New Brunswick (the Honourable Graydon Nicholas, 2009–2014) have all had Indigenous representatives of the Queen. All of these lieutenant governors used their time in office to highlight Indigenous issues, as well as to engage Canadians in First Nations' issues and in their shared history.

Lieutenant governors are appointed by governors general on the recommendation of prime ministers. Paradoxically, while the country has experienced for some time terrible federal/First Nations relations, it is the various prime ministers of the day (Pierre Trudeau, Brian Mulroney, Jean Chrétien, and Stephen Harper) who must be credited for the vice-regal appointments of Indigenous representatives of the Queen in the provinces.

Leading the negotiations during the 1990s that vindicated Louis Riel and transformed him from an outlaw to a Canadian founding father, Métis

W. Yvon Dumont was also the founding vice-president of the Native Council of Canada (today known as the Congress of Aboriginal Peoples (CAP)), president of both the Manitoba Métis Federation and the Métis National Council, and one of four Indigenous leaders that participated in the Charlottetown Accord. At the time of his vice-regal appointment, Dumont was suing Ottawa over five hundred thousand hectares of land in the Red River Valley promised to the Métis in the 1870s, and had no intention of stepping away from the lawsuit.

"I wouldn't have accepted the position if I thought I was going to have to give up a fight on behalf of the Métis people to which I have devoted years of my life," the lieutenant governor–designate told the *Windspeaker* newspaper.[38]

Dumont's swearing-in as Manitoba's twenty-first lieutenant governor on March 5, 1993, affirmed the Métis as a distinct and active part of Canadian society. Adding to the historic nature of Dumont's appointment was the fact that his office descended from that of the lieutenant governor of Rupert's Land and the Northwest Territories, an office once held by Red River Rebellion antagonist Sir William McDougall.[39]

When the Honourable James K. Bartleman was installed as the first Indigenous lieutenant governor of Ontario in 2002, he made fighting racism and discrimination, as well as Indigenous literacy, areas of focus for his mandate. Two years later, Bartleman launched the Lieutenant Governor's Book Drive, collecting 1.2 million books for Indigenous schools and Native Friendship Centres throughout Ontario. Bartleman also used his office to help establish a twinning program for Native and non-Native schools in Ontario and Nunavut, as well as founding four Indigenous literacy programs, which ultimately merged into the highly successful Lieutenant Governor's Aboriginal Summer Reading Camps.[40]

On December 6, 2007, James Bartleman was given the unprecedented honour of being invited to address the legislature at Queen's Park to launch a second book drive for Indigenous youth. Bartleman used the opportunity to recognize and thank Ontario Regional Chief Stan Beardy, as well as speak about his own observations of life in the First Nations communities he had visited across the province. Thanks to his skillful engagement of the vice-regal office, Bartleman pushed Indigenous issues of poverty, literacy, and mental illness into the consciousness of

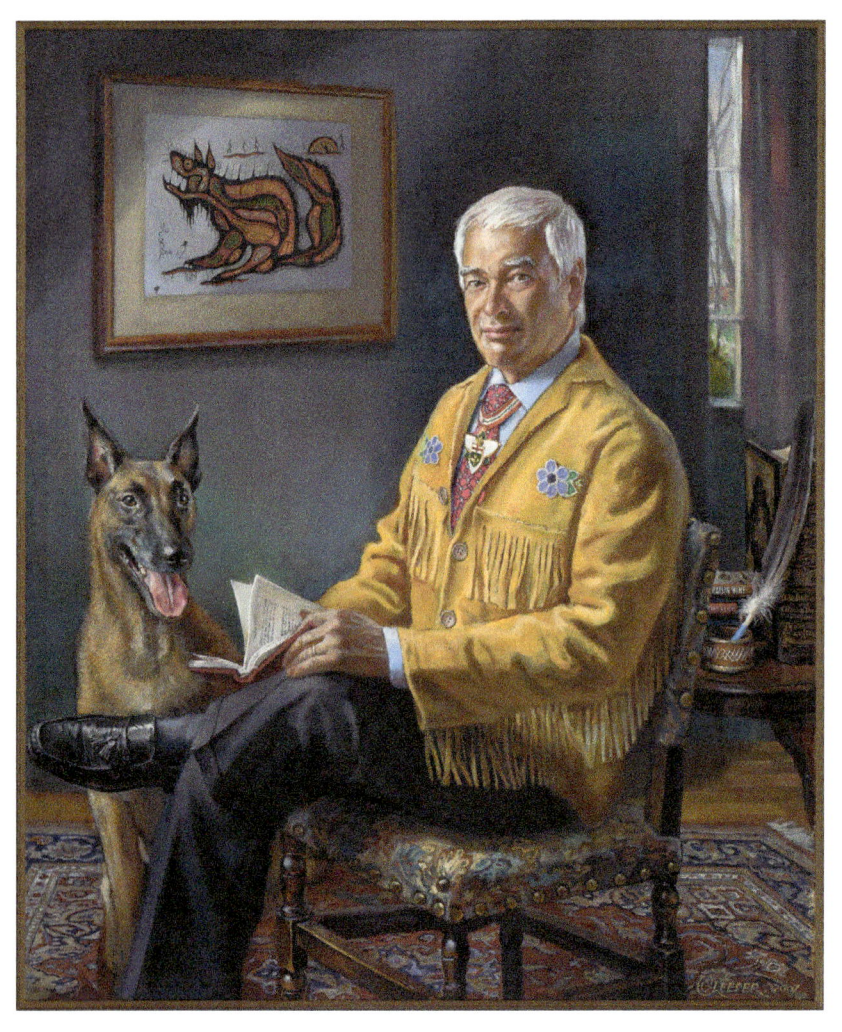

The Honourable James K. Bartleman, twenty-seventh lieutenant governor of Ontario and a member of the Chippewas of Mnjikaning (Rama) First Nation. *Courtesy of the Office of the Lieutenant Governor of Ontario.*

Ontarians and made meaningful, positive change in those areas. David Onley, Bartleman's successor continued to champion the Indigenous community, furthering the process of translating a historic relationship into a relevant and mutually productive one.

British Columbia's beloved Steven L. Point (a member of the Stó:lō Nation) made reconciliation one of the themes of his vice-regal mandate. Approachable and well spoken, Point went beyond speeches and vice-regal visits, actively working to bridge the Indigenous and non-Indigenous worlds embodied by his appointment.

In 2010, with the help of master carver Chief Tony Hunt, Point created a dug-out cedar canoe on the grounds of Victoria's Government House. Point later presented the canoe (highlighting the importance of gift-giving) to the people of British Columbia, saying, "*Shxwtitostel* [the name means "a safe place to cross the river"] is a gift to all peoples in British Columbia as a symbol of my belief that we need to create a better understanding amongst all people that we are in the same canoe. No matter where you are from, we all need to paddle together."[41]

The two carvers later worked together to recreate *Hosaqami*, a pole originally given life by Chief Hunt's adoptive grandfather, Mungo Martin, as a gift from the Royal Canadian Navy to the Royal Navy in 1959. While the original once stood at the British naval base at Whale Island, Portsmouth, the pole made by the lieutenant governor and chief would be raised on the grounds of Government House. Before he encouraged children from the five hundred people gathered to watch the raising of *Hosaqami* on September 8, 2012, Lieutenant Governor Point again restated his maxim: "… we have to, in this time and age, find a way to paddle together in one canoe."[42] The many hands that joined together to hoist the 7.3 metre pole into the sky gave life to the lieutenant governor's words.

Another of the many initiatives begun by Point was the founding of the 2924 (Khowutzun) Army Cadet Corps in Duncan, B.C., which blends Indigenous customs and practices with the National Army Cadet Program. Such efforts by Point affirm the assertions of his wife, Gwendolyn, at the time of her husband's appointment that it would be good for Indigenous peoples to have him as lieutenant governor. This seems like a significant understatement when considering the remarkable service the Honourable Steven Point did for British Columbia, highlighting the Indigenous community as an integral part of the province and the nation.

At his installation on September 30, 2009, the Honourable Grayden Nicholas swore allegiance to Queen Elizabeth II as Queen of Canada, then ascended to the highest office in New Brunswick holding an eagle feather (raising it high when he was proclaimed lieutenant governor to the cheers of the assembled crowd). In his installation speech, Nicholas, a member of the Maliseet Nation, first addressed the dignitaries in his Native tongue; then, in English, he spoke of his attendance at a sacred ceremony in a sweat lodge at the St. Mary's First Nation the day before to ask for prayers and support from the community. Nicholas spoke, too, of a sunrise ceremony held earlier that day near a great pine tree on the grounds of New Brunswick's Government House. It was not lost on the chiefs, elders, and other Indigenous attendees that most of Graydon Nicholas's actions and remarks that historic day would have been illegal a short time before under the Indian Act. Nicholas's speech as the thirtieth official representative of the Queen in New Brunswick was a powerful statement of truth and existence, fusing the Maliseet and Dignified Crown into one person.

A dramatic reminder of the line between the Dignified and Efficient Crowns in New Brunswick came on January 16, 2013, when Nicholas met, embraced, and danced with Indigenous protestors during the Idle No More movement's national "Day of Action."[43] When asked by reporters what he would do for the protestors, the lieutenant governor explained, "What I told them I would do is that I would act as a conduit, a medium for them. I knew information was going to be passed on to us. As I told them, [in] my position as the Lieutenant Governor of this province I would pass it on to the appropriate levels of government."[44]

Real and meaningful work is also being done by the Queen's non-Indigenous representatives in the twenty-first century, as their offices actively re-engage with the First Nations connected with their jurisdictions across the country.

In his opening address to the 2012 Crown/First Nations gathering held in Ottawa, Governor General David Johnston began his speech by acknowledging both the Treaty of Niagara and the Covenant Chain (such recognition was noticeably absent in 2014). His Excellency spoke to the gathered dignitaries, saying, "This gathering today is the modern version of that important council. And we have an opportunity to continue restoring the trust we have lost through the mistakes of the past." Concluding his remarks, Johnston declared the gathering open with the invocation, "Let us strengthen and burnish the Covenant Chain that binds us, and pledge to renew our dreams together."[45]

The governor general's remarks acknowledged that before the opening ceremonies a replica of the 1764 Covenant Chain Wampum had been displayed by Anishinaabe leaders, including Chief Isadore Day of the Serpent River First Nation, to the Assembly of First Nations' national chief, the prime minister, and a federal representative of the Queen. The wampum had originally been displayed backwards to show that, in Chief Day's words, "there's unfinished business and there's problems in the relationship," but was righted following smudging, prayers, and an exchange of gifts.[46]

Nova Scotia's lieutenant governor has had a difficult relationship with the Mi'kmaq people ever since Governor Cornwallis issued a proclamation in 1749, offering "… ten Guineas for every Indian Micmac taken or killed, to be paid upon producing such Savage taken or his scalp (as is the custom of America)." Within three years, this policy reduced the Indigenous population of the region by a devastating 80 percent, ensuring centuries of mistrust and hatred by the Mi'kmaq Nation toward the Dignified Crown in that province.[47] However, the repugnance of Cornwallis's proclamation serves to emphasize how remarkable the new and strong relationship (grounded in respect) that has recently been fostered between the modern vice-regal office and the Mi'kmaq Nation.

Brigadier General the Honourable J.J. Grant became the first vice-regal representative in modern Nova Scotia to host the grand chief and grand keptin of the Mi'kmaq Grand Council at his installation in 2012. This invitation reflected the historic link between the Mi'kmaq and the Crown, celebrated every year on October 1 (Treaty Day). Proclaimed in 1986, Treaty Day commemorates the Treaty of 1752 and, in the words of

The Honourable John James Grant, brigadier general (retired), CMM, ONS, CD, lieutenant governor of Nova Scotia, helps Jaden MacDonald and Arden Bernard hoist the Mi'kmaq flag over Halifax's Government House October 1, 2014. *Courtesy of Paula Raymond.*

Grand Chief Donald Marshall Sr., "… the unique and special relationship that exists between the Mi'kmaq and [H]er Majesty."[48] One of the many events that happen around Treaty Day in Nova Scotia sees the lieutenant governor raise the flag of the Mi'kmaq Nation over Government House (where it stays flying for the month). Later in the day, the lieutenant governor travels to the legislature to present awards to members of the Mi'kmaq community in a ceremony that includes prayers, speeches, and the annual submission to the Crown delivered by the grand keptin.

A similar event took place in Saskatchewan on October 25, 2013, when Lieutenant Governor Vaughn Solomon Schofield witnessed the raising of the Métis and Treaty Six flags over Saskatoon City Hall. In her remarks, the lieutenant governor recalled the meeting between Alexander Morris (her predecessor) and chiefs Mistawasis and Ahtahkakoop, adding, "It's no wonder that when the government shamefully neglected its responsibilities to the Treaties, some First Nations joined with the Métis in the Northwest Resistance."

Commenting on the importance of the flags being flown over Saskatoon City Hall, Her Honour said:

> Flags are powerful symbols. To have the Treaty 6 and Métis flags flown here, before City Hall, makes an important statement. It honours Saskatchewan's founding nations; it acknowledges that we are standing on Treaty 6 land; it shows respect for the contributions of First Nations and Métis peoples; it acknowledges that when we come together, we are so much stronger; and the flags hold the promise of a bright future for all.[49]

With Saskatchewan's rapidly growing Indigenous populations (one-third of the province will come from the Indigenous community by 2045[50]), the lieutenant governors of Saskatchewan have been uniquely positioned to rebuild community. Events have been organized that have included a historic meeting hosted by Lieutenant Governor Lynda Haverstock on May 10, 2006, that included Governor General Michaëlle Jean and all thirteen female First Nations chiefs from across the province. Similarily, Lieutenant Governor Gordon Barnhart hosted the opening of Sasipenita: The Recognition of Place, an exhibition highlighting the strength and endurance of Indigenous women. The current representative of the Queen has participated in a sweat lodge, attended pow wows, toured Indigenous communities in the north of the province, and brought greetings on behalf of the Queen to the various Treaty gatherings.

The 2014 North American Indigenous Games held in Regina provided an opportunity for the vice-regal official to demonstrate the role that the Dignified Crown can play in showing respect, bridging the gulf so often experienced between Indigenous peoples and Canada. The use of symbols — as highlighted in the lieutenant governor's earlier speech at the Saskatoon City Hall flag raising — both acknowledged and subtly reinforced the Treaty relationship, as well as the Queen's place at its very heart. As the senior official presiding over the ceremony, Solomon Schofield took the opportunity to welcome the athletes via video, in the name of the Queen, to Treaty Four Territory. Sitting at her desk at Government House with a portrait of the Queen and Prince Philip looking on and an eagle feather placed before her, the lieutenant governor, occasionally speaking in the Cree language, closed her address with greetings on behalf of "Her Majesty, Queen Elizabeth II, Queen of Canada."[51]

Prince Edward Island, Canada's "cradle of Confederation," has seen the fostering of a strong relationship between the island's Dignified Crown and Mi'kmaq peoples in recent times. In July 2010, Lieutenant Governor Barbara Hagerman participated in the annual St. Anne's Sunday, a popular event at Lennox Island Mi'kmaq First Nation, which coincided with the two-hundredth anniversary of St. Anne's Church and the four-hundredth anniversary of the baptism of Grand Chief Membertou (Queen Elizabeth II also participated in events to commemorate Membertou during her 2010 visit to Halifax). Hagerman's participation in that event and her efforts to highlight Prince Edward Island's cultural diversity, including hosting a celebration of Mi'kmaq culture at Fanningbank (Charlottetown's Government House), were acknowledged by Chief Darlene Bernard (the first Indigenous Islander to be inducted into the Order of Prince Edward Island in 2011) with the gift of a bald eagle feather on Treaty Day (October 1, 2008).

Hagerman's successor, the Honourable H. Frank Lewis, has continued to strengthen the relationship between his office and Indigenous Islanders. During a commemoration and reconciliation ceremony honouring former students of the Indian Residential School System held on the grounds of Province House, Lieutenant Governor Lewis sent a message calling for action in reconciliation. Lewis and his wife meet regularly with members of the Island Indigenous community, participate in ceremonies that include raising the Mi'kmaq flag over Government House, and have attended events such as St. Anne's Sunday.

Echoing the importance of gift-giving and tangible links to the Covenant Chain relationship in the Maritimes, a watch given by Queen Victoria to Lennox Island's famous Mi'kmaq teacher and First World War veteran John J. Sark was brought to Fanningbank when Frank Lewis presented Chief Bernard and Chief Francis with Diamond Jubilee Medals in 2012.

Nor is this relationship only an official one. Highlighting the meaningful and personal bond that has developed between the Crown in Prince Edward Island and the Indigenous community, Mrs. Lewis relayed to me how touched she was when both Chief Darlene Bernard and Chief Brian Francis attended the funeral of her father.

Building on the Indigenous youth literacy initiatives begun by the Honourable James K. Bartleman, David C. Onley, the twenty-eighth lieutenant governor of Ontario, founded a series of Aboriginal forums where Indigenous and non-Indigenous people could meet and share ideas. Interviewed by the *Toronto Star* in 2013, Onley explained his idea: "It is not up to people outside of First Nations — no matter how well-meaning — to impose solutions, but I believe this forum will help us identify the main challenges and how First Nations might go about tackling them, with our help where it is deemed necessary and welcome."[52]

Requiring the use of a scooter, David Onley was not able to visit most of Ontario's Indigenous fly-in communities. Recognizing the importance of personal contact between the vice-regal office and First Nations, Ruth Ann Onley often stood in for her husband. In this effort, Mrs. Onley visited twenty-three Indigenous literacy camps and thirteen communities, along with such vice-regal companions as Her Excellency Sharon Johnston, wife of the governor general, and the Honourable James Bartleman. Mrs. Onley's historic final tour in northern Ontario (discussed in Chapter Four) included the Countess of Wessex, Premier Kathleen Wynne, and the lieutenant governor–designate, Ms. Elizabeth Dowdeswell.

For his work in polishing the Covenant Chain of Friendship, David Onley was presented an eagle feather by Fort Albany Elder Andrew Wesley on September 10, 2014.

At the end of David Onley's time in vice-regal office, an "End of Mandate Report" was issued to highlight the hard work done by the Queen's provincial representative. The report included a prominent section under the heading "Aboriginal People in Ontario," explaining:

> Ontario's Aboriginal peoples have long had a special relationship with the Crown. Through his commitment to continue and expand the Aboriginal youth literacy initiatives of his predecessor, the Hon. James K. Bartleman, Mr. Onley — with the enthusiastic and invaluable assistance of his wife Ruth Ann — made a lasting contribution to strengthening this bond.[53]

Vice-Regal Honorary Witnesses to the Truth and Reconciliation:

- the Right Honourable Michaëlle Jean, governor general of Canada (2009)
- the Honourable David Onley, lieutenant governor of Ontario (2011)
- Mrs. Gwendolyn Point (2012)
- the Honourable Philip S. Lee, lieutenant governor of Manitoba (2012)
- the Honourable Judith Guichon, lieutenant governor of British Columbia (2013)
- the Honourable Steven Point, former lieutenant governor of British Columbia (2013)
- the Right Honourable David Johnston, governor general of Canada (2014)

Of the nearly sixty Honorary Witnesses to the five years of hearings of the Indian Residential School Truth and Reconciliation Commission, seven have been vice-regal representatives or their spouses (including both the first witness, Governor General Michaëlle Jean, and one of the last, Governor General David Johnston). Continuing the work of her predecessor, British Columbia's current lieutenant governor, the Honourable Judith Guichon, also became an Honorary Witness of Truth and Reconciliation Commission at a ceremony in Government House and subsequently participated in five days of events for the Truth and Reconciliation Commission's national event in Vancouver in 2013. She also took part in the 2013 "Walk for Reconciliation" in Vancouver along with Chief Ian Campbell, one of the sixteen hereditary chiefs of the Squamish Nation, Assembly of First Nations National Chief Shawn Atleo, the previous lieutenant governor, Steven L. Point, and thousands of marchers.

Mrs. Gwendolyn Point, the Honourable Judith Guichon, lieutenant governor of British Columbia, and the Honourable Steven Point, former lieutenant governor of British Columbia, at the 2013 Walk for Reconciliation in Vancouver. Seventy thousand people from all walks of life, including then-National Chief Shawn Atleo, Dr. Bernice King (Dr. Martin Luther King's daughter), Vancouver mayor Gregor Robertson, and many First Nations' leaders participated in that remarkable event held on a rainy September 22, 2013. *Courtesy of the Office of the Lieutenant Governor of British Columbia.*

I was interested to learn during my research for this book of a 2010 plan to make the Countess of Wessex an Honorary Witness. When floated to the various communities involved with the commission (this, of course, included its Indigenous members), the idea of appointing a Royal witness was universally applauded. When the idea reached the Canadian government, however, it advised that such an invitation should not be extended. While it was acceptable to have two governors general, as well as a handful of lieutenant governors, as part of the Truth and Reconciliation Commission, a member of the Royal Family would not be approved by the Government of Canada.

While such roadblocks exist, members of the Royal Family, including Queen Elizabeth II herself, continue to honour their historic relationships with Indigenous peoples across the continent. Nearly every Royal Tour of the country by members of the Royal Family involves interacting with the Indigenous community. Recent examples that highlight the personal bond between the Dignified Crown and First Nations include the Duke and Duchess of Cambridge meeting Wendake Grand Chief Konrad Sioui before departing HMCS *Montreal* for Quebec City (2011), the Prince of Wales's meeting with the Assembly of First Nations (2012), and the Princess Royal being given the Anishinaabe name "Ogimaa Kwens" (meaning "Little Royal Lady" — both Queen Victoria and Elizabeth II are named "Ogimaa Kwe" or "Royal Lady") in Winnipeg (1999).

An especially poignant moment occurred in 2010 during a visit to St. James's Cathedral in Toronto by the Queen, who presented representatives of the Mohawks of the Bay of Quinte and Six Nations of the Grand River with two sets of silver hand bells. The gift commemorated the delegation of "Four Indian Kings" that met with Queen Anne,[54] "with the usual Ceremonies due to foreign Heads, and their Embassadors [sic],"[55] on April 19, 1710.

In a meeting that included the exchange of wampum, a three-hundred-year personal relationship was forged between the Monarch and the Haudenosaunee Confederacy. Commenting on the recent British victories against the French (referred to as "Canada") during Queen Anne's War (1702–1713), the delegation (through a translator) declared:

> The Reduction of Canada is of such Weight, that after the effecting thereof, we should have *free Hunting*, and a great Trade with our *Great Queen's* Children: And as a Token of the Sincerity of the Six Nations, we do here, in the Names of all, present our *Great Queen* with these Belts of *Wampum*.[56]

THE QUEEN AT THE COUNCIL FIRE

In response to the address, Queen Anne promised to send them a missionary, leading to the construction of a chapel in the Mohawk Valley the following year (it would be rebuilt along the Grand River in 1784 following the American Revolution). Anne also supplied the newly built chapel with a double set of communion silver, as well as a reed organ in 1711. It should be noted that the present Queen has only two Royal Chapels outside of the United Kingdom,[57] and both are on Mohawk territory and filled with centuries of gifts from the Royal Family.[58] The 1711 silverware presented by Queen Anne is still in use, and was proudly on display at the 250th anniversary commemorations of the Treaty of Niagara.

Royal Arms and cypher of Queen Anne etched into the silver flagon presented by her to the Mohawk Nation that was displayed August 2, 2014, at the 250th anniversary commemorations of the Treaty of Niagara by the Anishinaabe and Haudenosaunee nations. The flagon is currently held with half of the Queen Anne Silver at Christ Church, Her Majesty's Royal Chapel of the Mohawks, in the Tyendinaga Mohawk Territory. The other half of the Queen Anne Silver is kept by Her Majesty's Royal Chapel of the Mohawks in the territory of the Six Nations on the Grand River. *Courtesy of author.*

## THE QUEEN AT THE COUNCIL FIRE

The hand bells presented by the Queen in 2010 were engraved with the words "The Silver Chain of Friendship 1710–2010" — a direct reference to the Covenant Chain.

"It was [the Queen's] idea," Chief R. Donald Maracle said. "She wanted to honour the anniversary. We're pleased that she remembers the Mohawk people and our mutual history for the past three centuries."[59]

Writing about the event in *Turtle Island News*, editor Lynda Powless remarked that "Queen Elizabeth II, in the spirit of her ancestors, came to Canada bearing gifts for the Royal Chapels of the Mohawks, here at Six Nations and at Tyendinaga.… It was an honourable moment.…" Powless went on to say, "… the Confederacy Council had been writing to her for years saying it was time to re-polish the chain of friendship."[60]

Two years after this important gift acknowledged the Covenant Chain, the Prince of Wales met with Indigenous leaders at the Fairmount Royal York in Toronto, where he was presented with an eagle feather by Grand Chief David Harper of Manitoba Keewatinowi Okimakanak. He was also

The Royal Arms presented to the Mohawk Chapel by King George III. Carved out of a single piece of oak, the arms remain in pristine condition in the little wooden chapel (Ontario's oldest Protestant church). *Courtesy Her Majesty's Royal Chapel of the Mohawks.*

shown a replica of the 1764 Covenant Chain Wampum and informed of its meaning by Grand Chief Patrick Mahdabee, who reminded the prince that "England was not off the hook yet," and that Canada and Britain were still bound by the obligations made at Niagara.[61]

During this meeting, the chiefs requested an audience with the Queen to commemorate the 250th anniversary of the proclamation, as well as ask why Canada had failed to honour the treaties signed afterwards. The Prince assured the chiefs that he would pass on the message to the Queen, but no such meeting was organized.[62]

As Prince of Wales, Charles has long represented his mother, often standing in for the Dignified Crown during key anniversaries and events since his first Royal Tour of Canada in 1970.

In 1977, Prince Charles represented the Queen at centenary commemorations for the signing of Treaty Seven with the Blackfoot Confederacy. Travelling to Blackfoot Crossing, Alberta, the prince visited reserves, hearing about the different issues affecting the people. After being in Blackfoot Crossing for two days, Charles was given an Indigenous name (Red Crow — a name shared with Chief Mékaisto, a prominent signatory of Treaty Seven, and a previous Prince of Wales, the future Edward VIII), as he witnessed a re-enactment of the actual signing, distributing medallions to commemorate his participation.

On April 8, 2001, the Prince of Wales held a private reception at Wanuskewin Heritage Park near Saskatoon, Saskatchewan, attended by many Indigenous dignitaries and community members. Chief Perry Bellegarde, of the Federation of Saskatchewan Indian Nations, was the first to greet the prince, presenting him with both a star blanket and Treaty booklet. Bellegarde later commented that the gathering was "an important and highly symbolic gathering at Wanuskewin. It demonstrates to His Royal Highness not only the historical significance of the Treaties, but the fact that even today First Nation peoples remain loyal to the Treaties and the nation to nation relationship with the Monarchy."[63]

## THE QUEEN AT THE COUNCIL FIRE

Every First Nation representative had a personal meeting with the Prince of Wales to discuss the importance of treaties and their connections with the Crown. At the end of the visit, Charles was given the name Pisimwa Kamiwohkitahpamikohk (meaning, "The sun looks at him in a good way") by Gordon Oakes, elder and past chief of the Nekaneet Nation. Oakes explained, "HRH Prince Charles is the Queen's [Victoria] great-great grandson and that made giving him this name so very important to First Nations peoples."[64] The prince has been given other Indigenous names, including Leading Star by Cree and Ojibwe students in 1996, and Attaniout Ikeneego (meaning, "Son of the Big Boss" in Inuktitut) in 2001.

The visit to Wanuskewin ended with a private walk with Elder Ben Weenie (Stoney Knoll First Nation) which, according to the newspaper

The Prince of Wales, wearing a star blanket, is escorted by Chief Perry Bellegarde and Elder Gordon Oakes (foreground) at Wanuskewin Heritage Park in Treaty Six territory, Saskatchewan, on April 28, 2001. *Courtesy of the Government of Saskatchewan.*

*Saskatchewan Indian*, included discussions around treaties, Indigenous customs, and traditions. The paper noted, "The [p]rince even acknowledged some of his beliefs related to First Nation's connection to the land."[65] This last point is significant due to the Prince's keen interest in environmental sustainability — many of Charles's areas of interest intersect with those of Indigenous peoples across the continent (see His Royal Highness's 2010 manifesto *Harmony*).

Prince's Charities Canada (PCC), established to support the charitable work and core interests of the Prince of Wales, makes it a point to highlight that "[t]he Crown and First Nations communities have a close association dating centuries before the creation of Canada." Under the heading "Aboriginal Initiatives," the organization explains that Charles has an interest in developing this association further: "While HRH The Prince of Wales has many official opportunities to work with Canada's Aboriginal communities, he is keen to connect with First Nations on a more personal level through his charitable work."[66]

The Prince's hope to connect with Indigenous peoples has led to numerous initiatives, including a partnership between the First Nations University of Canada and The Prince's School of Traditional Arts in London (UK). In 2014, artist and professor of fine arts Judy Anderson (of the First Nations University) taught a semester at The Prince's School of Traditional Arts, before hosting the Prince of Wales at a traditional beading and quilling workshop at the Dulwich Picture Gallery in South London. The PCC's support of Indigenous art has also lead to the kindling of a relationship between The Prince's School of Traditional Arts and the Ahousaht First Nation in British Columbia to revitalize traditional craft amongst young people.

Other relationships developed by the Prince include an Indigenous hiring initiative run under the banner of the Prince's Canadian Responsible Business Network, which places urban Indigenous youth in sustainable jobs. The PCC recently facilitated a partnership between the One Laptop per Child Foundation (based in Cambridge, Massachusetts) and Indigenous-language publisher SayITFirst to help with the distribution of content written in traditional languages. The Prince's Charities Canada is also working to include traditional language curriculum in Frontier College's summer literacy camps.

The Prince of Wales's son, Prince William, the Duke of Cambridge, has also done much to maintain the bond between the Crown and Indigenous peoples in Canada. In 2001, the Duke and Duchess of Cambridge took part in a prayer and welcome song by Dene drummers in Yellowknife, Northwest Territories. During his address afterward, the Duke responded to the drummers by saying "thank you" in both Dene and Inuvialuktun. Both the Duke and Duchess are honorary Canadian Rangers (a sub-component of the Canadian Armed Forces Reserve largely made up of Indigenous members) — the Duke was made a

The Prince of Wales learns about beading and quilling from Judy Anderson, a professor of fine arts at the First Nations University, during his November 11, 2014, visit to the Dulwich Picture Gallery in South London. Anderson taught the Prince to attach beads and quills to a moose hide during a Royal Visit that included meetings with other Native artists. *Courtesy of the Prince's Charities Canada.*

Ranger with his brother, Prince Harry, in 2009, and the Duchess was inducted during her tour in 2011.

Other members have been active, too. Witnessed by Lieutenant Governor Gordon Barnhart and the Treaty Four chiefs at Regina's Government House in 2007, Anne, the Princess Royal, faced all four directions with the elders as Elder Margaret Keewatin called out her new Cree name, Wapis-ki-mahehkan-iskwew (meaning "White Wolf Woman"). After the naming ceremony, Anne was draped in a satin and silk shawl decorated with intricate beading and ribbons.

Prince Edward, the Earl of Wessex, took part in the 2003 Prince Albert Urban Treaty Day commemorations (including a re-enactment of the 1876 signing of Treaty Six) before opening the First Nations University of Canada, North America's first all-Aboriginal university. The Earl and Countess of Wessex's extensive work on behalf of First Nations is explored in greater detail in Chapter Four.

Even Canada's Royal symbols have highlighted the Monarch's relationship with Indigenous peoples, ensuring the inclusion of Indigenous symbols within contemporary Canadian icons. While most Canadians do not realize that the "Canadian coat of arms" is in fact the Arms of Her Majesty the Queen in Right of Canada (the Queen is the personification of the Canadian State), the fact that the heraldic symbol of Canada is that of the Queen herself is likely not lost on Indigenous peoples.

Interestingly, while Her Majesty's Arms in Right of Canada are devoid of Indigenous symbols, the provincial arms offer numerous examples. The Queen's Arms in Right of Manitoba include a horse supporter wearing "a Collar of Prairie Indian beadwork" supporting a medallion, while the arms of New Brunswick include a white-tailed deer with a collar of Maliseet friendship wampum. Similar to Manitoba, both of the supporters of the arms used in Saskatchewan wear collars of beadwork (one of them supporting the province's Order of Merit). Two Beothuk supporters "garbed for war proper" can be found in the Queen's

The Queen's Arms in Right of Saskatchewan. Notice that the supporters wear collars of Native beadwork. *Courtesy of the Government of Saskatchewan.*

Arms in Right of Newfoundland and Labrador, and Her Majesty's Nova Scotia arms (the oldest grant of arms in the Commonwealth outside the United Kingdom) depict a "17th-century representation of the North American Indian."[67]

Looking at the evolution of Canadian heraldry, a prerogative of the Crown, over the twenty-five years since the founding of the Canadian Heraldic Authority, a prolific use of Indigenous imagery can be seen. This has occurred in consultation with First Nations, and has resulted in such wonderful creations as the beautiful and distinctive arms of Nunavut.

Despite the fact that most Canadians lack any real understanding of the significance of the treaties signed on behalf of the Crown in this country or of the nature of the Dignified Crown — its personal relationship with First Nations peoples as well as the institution's function as a whole — the two continue to be in relationship. Working within constitutionally grey areas, the Dignified Crown continues to maintain its relationship with Indigenous peoples, whether it is during the confines of a Royal Tour, or through the mandates of vice-regal officials. However, a consequence of our compound constitutional monarchy has been a fragmentation of this relationship. The strength of the effort extended on behalf of the Dignified Crown largely depends on the person who holds the office — that and how the convention of responsible government is used by the government of the day. With all of this in mind, much can still be done to polish the Covenant Chain and walk with Indigenous peoples on a path toward reconciliation, but this future is one that must include the Queen and her official representatives in Canada.

CHAPTER FOUR

# Building Community — A Model Royal Visit

During the final week of the mandate of Ontario lieutenant governor David C. Onley, an extraordinary Royal visit took place in the fly-in Indigenous community of Kitchenuhmaykoosib Inninuwug (KI). On September 18 and 19, a delegation of high-profile women invited by the Countess of Wessex (daughter-in-law to the Queen) departed Nipissing University and landed in northern Ontario, creating what should become a template for future Royal Tours across the country. Rather than simply pausing for a brief stop during a day of events in the region, the Royal party stayed the night in the reserve, sleeping in people's homes across the community. (The ceremonial guards slept on the floor of one of the residences.) Joining the Countess were Ruth Ann Onley (the tireless wife of the outgoing lieutenant governor), Premier Kathleen Wynne, Lieutenant Governor–designate Elizabeth Dowdeswell, Vicki Hayman (the wife of the U.S. ambassador), and various other leaders from corporate, academic, and philanthropic spheres in the province. Many more wanted to be there, but had to be turned away due to the logistics of the visit and accommodations available at KI.

Ontario premier Kathleen Wynne, Ontario lieutenant governor–designate Elizabeth Dowdeswell, and the Countess of Wessex were made honorary members of the Canadian Rangers during their visit to Kitchenuhmaykoosib Inninuwug (KI) in September 2014. These women join Ruth Ann Onley to make up the only four honorary rangers in the province of Ontario. *Courtesy of the Office of the Lieutenant Governor of Ontario.*

This was not the Countess's first visit to a First Nation. The Earl and Countess of Wessex's extensive working visits to the country usually and deliberately include purposeful and meaningful encounters with Indigenous peoples. At the insistence of the Royal couple, their work in Canada has specifically included meetings with commissioners of the Truth and Reconciliation Commission and residential school survivors.

The 2014 Royal visit to Kitchenuhmaykoosib Inninuwug acknowledged an open call issued the previous year by the youth of the community for Canadians to come and visit their home during National Aboriginal Week. After an invitation by Lieutenant Governor David Onley for the Royal couple to visit a fly-in community in northern Ontario, Her Royal Highness's Canadian lady-in-waiting, Tania

Carnegie, travelled to KI to learn more about the First Nation. One year later, the Countess of Wessex arrived, bringing with her a delegation of leaders. Her Royal Highness's time in northern Ontario was part of a larger working visit by the Earl and Countess centred on their intention to educate themselves about Indigenous issues across the country.

The tour began in British Columbia with a First Nations round-table dinner at Government House, a meeting where Indigenous leaders gathered and voiced their successes and concerns, revealing common themes that ran across the country. The notion of "respect" came about very early in their discussions.

When visiting the Ditidaht First Nation, the Royal couple and British Columbia's lieutenant governor, Judith Guichon, met with Ditidaht hereditary leaders, as well as the elected leadership, to ask permission to be on their lands. At the formal welcome to the community, Prince Edward explained that he brought greetings from "… his father, his mother, his grandparents, and great-grandparents." When the Countess was presented with a traditional cedar headband woven by Elder Fran Edgar ("… you wear our crown" was said as Lucy Edgar placed it on her head), Her Royal Highness kept it on for the entire visit (similar headbands were worn by the Prince of Wales and Duchess of Cornwall during their 2009 visit to Victoria). After a day of events that included the opening of a new library, a visit to the local RCMP station, and the Countess paddling in a traditional canoe, everyone gathered with the couple for a community feast.

Visiting the 'Namgis Nation on Cormorant Island the following day, the Royal couple visited the U'mista Cultural Centre, which held repatriated family masks and regalia that had been removed as a result of the laws banning potlatch ceremonies during the nineteenth and twentieth centuries. They then met with residential school survivors in front of the abandoned hulk of St. Michael's Indian Residential School at Alert Bay. The day was finished by joining the community at the 'Namgis Bighouse for traditional drumming and dancing where the earl and countess witnessed and participated in a community celebration.[1]

In KI it was no different. The Countess exchanged gifts with Chief Danny Morris, elders, and other community members, visiting the site with Premier Wynne and other dignitaries where the community signed Treaty Nine in 1929. Addressing the people, elders, council, and chief, Her Royal Highness evoked the historic relationship between the Dignified Crown and the KI Nation when she brought greetings on behalf of the "Great White Mother."

Ruth Ann Onley discussed the relationship between the Crown and Indigenous peoples in an op-ed published in the *Globe and Mail* on her husband's last day in the vice-regal office:

> Nurturing the relationship between the Crown and First Nations of Ontario is an ongoing concern for the Lieutenant Governor's office and a visit from a member of the Royal Family had huge significance, for the community and for future relations. The presence of the Countess of Wessex demonstrated to the community that they matter.[2]

What made the visit so significant was the fact that the Countess had become a catalyst — a Council Fire — that gathered influential people together with their Indigenous counterparts, providing real opportunity for new relationships to emerge and communities to grow. In such efforts, the community building nature of the Dignified Crown is unparalleled in Canada. An invitation by a member of the Royal Family, or their representatives, seldom goes unanswered, and having the Dignified Crown at an event undoubtedly attracts media attention. The Dignified Crown also brings a great deal of history with it, triggering complex feelings and memories. Acting as a nucleus for an event, however, the Dignified Crown and the stories and feelings it conjures for those connected with it have a natural tendency to bind people together

BUILDING COMMUNITY — A MODEL ROYAL VISIT

The Countess of Wessex and delegates attended an evening community celebration (which included a feast, fire, drumming, and circle dance) along the shores of Big Trout Lake during their historic visit to Kitchenuhmaykoosib Inninuwug. *Courtesy of the Office of the Lieutenant Governor of Ontario.*

in a shared experience. The Crown elevates events in a way that transcends pomp and ceremony, offering an opportunity to connect previously disconnected people.

While the Dignified Crown can no longer actively direct change, it can be the centre of an event that brings together those in power and the stakeholders who need their help to ensure that something meaningful happens.

The visitors stayed in KI for a significant amount of time, affording opportunities for shared experiences to develop and sink in. The attendance of the social, economic, and political movers of the province, as well as a member of the Royal Family, made the visit meaningful, and connected everyone in a powerful shared experience. The presence of David Onley's successor, Elizabeth Dowdeswell, assured the continuation of the work begun under the Honourable James Bartleman into the next viceregal mandate — corporate memory was being publicly assured.

The fact that this was a delegation of women was something that also resonated with the community. Women are the backbone of many Anishinaabe and other Indigenous communities and have long been honoured as teachers, nurturers, healers, and the memory holders of a Nation. That the Countess was surrounded by strong women displayed an understanding and respect of the Anishinaabe community. The meetings between the visitors and the female elders were sacred and fruitful, interactions that honoured the way the people of Kitchenuhmaykoosib Inninuwug have been discussing issues within their community for generations.

In some ways, the historic meeting at KI was what Chief Theresa Spence had been asking to happen in 2012–2013. Many will suggest that the only reason such an event happened was because it did so within the provincial realm. The Countess of Wessex was not "officially" representing the corporate Queen of Canada and the constitutional representative of the Dignified Crown in Ontario (the lieutenant governor) was not in KI. Her Royal Highness's visit was designated as a "working visit," and was funded by the private sector and not the federal government. While all of this may be true, the visit was no less important to the people of KI and the delegation that they hosted. The fact that it happened is what will be remembered.

"The original treaty signing in 1929 was also a 'Royal visit' because it included the King's representatives with whom they signed the treaty," one of the organizers reminded me, "thus this is considered the first Royal visit since the treaty signing. That's a rather complicated logic but it is how the community feels."[3] That the community's feelings were being acknowledged and respected is very important.

The Countess herself observed the importance of language and commented that people needed to "… stop, be still and listen …" to Indigenous communities. Her Royal Highness also wisely counselled, "We need to be mindful not to use words that imply meaning or expectations that cannot be met."[4]

"A word that came up many times, before, during and after our stay in KI was Reconciliation," explained Ruth Ann Onley. "In the context of our visit, rather than a transaction or a process, reconciliation meant dissolving a relationship that no longer works and building a new one, by watching, listening and bearing witness."[5]

Building on the spirit of Onley's words, the Countess continued her conversations with the Indigenous community beyond her time in Kitchenuhmaykoosib Inninuwug, addressing four hundred people (including Premier Wynne, Ontario Minister of Aboriginal Affairs David Zimmer, and Ontario Regional Chief Stan Beardy) at Nipissing University the day after her stay at the fly-in reserve. While her husband, the Earl of Wessex, attended events in Saskatchewan honouring the Whitecap Dakota First Nation's allied participation in the War of 1812, the Countess spoke of the pain endured by residential school survivors, the importance of preserving language, treaty rights, and her own pledge to help in any way that she could. Her Royal Highness finished her talk by saying:

The First Nations have a unique relationship with the Royal Family going back many years. This relationship has continued. Even today, our Queen is referred to as "The Great White Mother," and the enormous respect that she is held by the people of the First Nations remains. I hope that through my involvement with the proud Aboriginal People of this land the old bonds of our relationship are strengthened.[6]

The ever-evolving nature of our Confederation seems to be compensating for the breakdown of the federal Treaty relationship. The Countess of Wessex's official status in relation to the Canadian Crown was irrelevant to the members of KI; rather, what counted was that she was the wife of the Queen's youngest son. Whether or not treaties fall within the constitutional jurisdiction of the provinces, there is a consensus emerging in this country that new relationships are being forged using the Dignified Crown as a vehicle for communication and community.

In his 1985 article "Recognition in International Law," Douglas Sanders writes, "It is common wisdom that the queen … [is] powerless … [and, as a result] well-meaning advisors have in the past often tried to steer [First Nations] away from petitions to the crown." Sanders goes on to concede that only by ignoring such advice and forwarding their petitions and grievances have First Nations successfully initiated changes in the Canadian Constitution.[7] First Nations refusal to see the Crown as simply a ceremonial aspect of the state defies mainstream Canadian perceptions of their constitutional monarchy. While Canadian political scientists (and likely the federal government) will line up to challenge the Indigenous interpretation of the status and nature of the Dignified Crown, or the recent actions of the Countess of Wessex in Ontario, the point must be made that a one-way definition of the Crown no longer applies.

Interactions with the Dignified Crown begin as visceral experiences, but are now becoming practical relationships that are mutually

Lieutenant governor–designate Elizabeth Dowdeswell, Chief Danny Morris, the Countess of Wessex, and Ruth Ann Onley stand at the site where the community signed Treaty Nine in 1929. *Courtesy of the Office of the Lieutenant Governor of Ontario.*

beneficial. Recalling the visit to KI with the Countess, Ruth Ann Onley wrote:

> I am still processing the emotional aftermath of our visit to KI … but certain visuals stand out in my memory, foremost among them the Countess standing with a group of women elders, who had come to the airport to say goodbye and spontaneously began to sing "God Save The Queen," bringing her to the point of tears.

The final paragraph of Her Honour's article moves beyond such reflections to a more concrete definition of the "new relationship" as envisioned by Onley:

Our delegation — and especially the presence of the Countess of Wessex — demonstrated to the leadership, youth, and community of KI that people in the world beyond the reserve care about them and their future. By honouring their history and culture and, perhaps more importantly, by transmitting back to our own communities what we witnessed, our visit has begun a process we can build on, if we have the collective courage to do so.[8]

CHAPTER FIVE

# Suggestions for Moving Forward Together

As has been explored in earlier chapters, contemporary Canadians are comfortable with a distant Sovereign whose role is strictly limited by the conventions of constitutional monarchy, while many First Nations demand a more personal and engaged relationship with the Crown.

Respecting that personal relationship is key to reconciliation because it underscores the equality of First Nations with Canada (both the Dignified and Efficient Crown). This respect can be acknowledged through acts of recognition, gift-giving, communication, and other protocols that can only be done properly through the Dignified Crown. There are scores of issues that affect Indigenous peoples today: education, murdered or missing Indigenous women, poverty, environmental "development," et cetera. At the core of all of these critical areas remains the need for First Nations to be shown respect by the Canadian State (the Crown). The Dignified Crown is a vehicle that can do this on a regular basis — in some cases it already is.

The late twentieth and early twentieth-first centuries have witnessed the peeling away of the "Indian" label created by the 1876 Indian Act and the Indian Residential School System, revealing a diverse and distinct community of First Nations. The very idea of 630 or more individual nations existing in Canada is overwhelming for the Canadian government (hence the creation of the monolithic term "Indian" that persists today). This fact has unleashed a host of concerns over protocol and other issues surrounding individual Treaty relationships.

Interestingly, while the Canadian government still tries to deal with "Indians" as one block of North American society, the official representatives of the Queen of Canada (particularly those in the provinces) find themselves at the forefront of redefining relationships between Canada and Indigenous peoples. Indigenous and non-Indigenous lieutenant governors engaged in reconciliation have demonstrated a unique ability to recognize the diverse and complex societies that exist across their jurisdictions. Paradoxically, Canada's compound monarchy has allowed each provincial representative of the Queen (an official that has no formal relationship with First Nations laid out in our constitutional documents) to adapt and engage Indigenous peoples in meaningful and personal relationships. The ten different manifestations of the Queen of Canada that are created by the official representatives operating at the provincial level give the Crown in this country a remarkable amount of flexibility, allowing offices to evolve to meet the needs of their specific regions.

There are instances of the provincial Dignified Crowns tailoring their interactions with Indigenous peoples in a way that the federal government has yet to do, or is incapable of doing because of the constitutional implications placed on the Sovereign and governor general. Much of this has to do with the constitutional grey area in which lieutenant governors live in relation to Indigenous peoples — nothing they say or do is constitutionally binding.

However, as the idea of provincial and federal co-sovereignty develops in Canada, this may change. The Honourable Steven Point was quick to tell me, "The lieutenant governors do not kowtow to the governor general;"[1] rather they see themselves as co-equal partners with the federal government, not simply one level below them.

Again, I must stress, for Indigenous peoples it is the fact that the provincial vice-regals represent the Queen that is important and not their political and constitutional roles. The personal connection is key, not the political.

So much of how First Nations interact with one another and the environment is through personal relationships — the Crown (originally and deliberately presented in personal terms) is a vehicle through which such interactions can be re-established between First Nations and the Canadian State. Embracing the Dignified Crown's role as a link between non-Indigenous and Indigenous worlds does not mean abandoning responsible government, or any of our other constitutional realities. However, it does require non-Indigenous Canadians to allow the office of the Queen of Canada to rediscover this role and embrace the fact that personal relationships between the Monarch, her representatives, the Royal Family, and First Nations have a place in our Constitution and the Confederation it manifests.

Key areas should be addressed and developed as a means to restoring the principles of the Treaty of Niagara and Covenant Chain to the Dignified Crown.

### Respecting Protocol and the Crown's Corporate Memory Concerning Treaty Relationships

Acknowledging the importance of protocol in the minds of Indigenous peoples is critical to reconciliation. Each and every First Nation is a distinct entity and must be treated with a level of respect that only the Dignified Crown can offer. Examples of such interactions can be found in the relationships between the lieutenant governor of British Columbia and the region's Indigenous population.

Most First Nations in British Columbia recognize both hereditary leaders and elected chiefs. Traditionally, the hereditary chiefs never speak publicly; instead, they have designated speakers (who themselves occupy very dignified roles). Nonetheless, the hereditary chiefs occupy central roles within their Nations and are always consulted by the elected leadership. Observing such protocols within the Nation itself is key to ensuring that the community buys into the initiatives of its elected government.

Typically, for example, formal greetings by First Nations to federal or provincial representatives are always done by, or in the name of, the hereditary leaders. When the lieutenant governor engages with a particular Nation, she is sure to meet with both the hereditary and the elected leadership. These meetings tell the community that it is both respected and acknowledged as an equal.

James Hammond, private secretary to the lieutenant governor of British Columbia, informed me that "going through the step of greeting a lieutenant governor in regalia, speaking the Nation's language, and performing a welcome dance are all important steps for First Nations before they get down to discussions with government officials."[2]

The statement of acknowledgement of the traditional territory they are in made by members of the Royal Family and the official representatives of the Queen before delivering addresses or participating in ceremonies is an important protocol that is becoming common at events across the country. Such statements of acknowledgement should become a regular feature of Royal and vice-regal tours and events nationwide.

Looking across the globe to another Commonwealth realm, the governor general of New Zealand (also commonly referred to by his Māori title, *Te Kāwana Tianara o Aotearoa*),[3] provides numerous examples of practices that could be adopted by Canadian vice-regal offices. By integrating Indigenous languages, culture, and concepts (i.e., *mana*) into speeches, ensuring each address includes greetings in Māori (and other languages found in the realm), and being involved in important Māori events and traditions, the Dignified Crown of New Zealand has become a true community builder. There is no hint of tokenism in New Zealand's vice-regal office; rather, the Indigenous identity of the Dignified Crown is seamlessly woven in with its non-Indigenous aspects — the governor general moves easily between the different cultures he is in relationship with.

This new dimension of the New Zealand governor general began with the appointment of the Venerable and the Honourable Sir Paul Alfred Reeves in 1985. As the first Māori representative of the Queen of New Zealand, Reeves went a long way to reconcile a very complicated relationship begun with the Treaty of Waitangi (the 1840 Treaty between Queen Victoria and Māori leadership at the heart of the country's unwritten constitution). While Māori ceremonies had already been introduced to the State Opening of Parliament in 1984, Reeves gave such inclusions an element of legitimacy. Before becoming the Queen's representative, Reeves went to his people, the Te Āti Awa at Bell Block, Taranaki, to explain that he would accept a post that some thought no Māori had any business filling. For his installation, Sir Paul introduced the *nohoanga kainga*, a Māori ceremony of welcome on the grounds and within the walls of Wellington's Government House.

New Zealand's controversial Waitangi Day created tense moments for the Māori governor general, especially when he attended (against his government's advice) commemorations in 1987, and was present during the 1990 Royal Tour by the Queen (where a wet T-shirt was thrown at the Monarch). However, the seeds for a new, personal relationship between the Dignified Crown and the Māori had been sown. Currently, New Zealand has had two Māori governors general: Sir Paul Reeves (1985–1990) and Lt. Gen. the Rt. Hon. Sir Jerry Mateparae (2011–present day).

While the New Zealand model might be more difficult for the Canadian governor general to follow due to the country's immense size and the numerous First Nations with their own relationships (or lack thereof) with the Crown, the Kiwi Crown could be very informative for the provincial vice-regal offices. Both the New Zealand and Canadian Dignified Crowns have similar starting points: New Zealand's 1840 Treaty of Waitangi, and the various treaties in North America with the British and Canadian Crowns created personal relationships between both sovereigns (Elizabeth II as Queen of New Zealand and Queen of Canada) and the Indigenous Nations that share their lands. It is important to note that while informative, the New Zealand relationship is not perfect. It has developed through some very difficult times — most notably the 1995 Waitangi Day commemorations which saw Māori Hinewhare Harawira spit in the face of Governor General Dame Catherine Tizard.

However, 1995 was also the year of a significant, and possibly instructive, event in the life of the Pacific realm, thanks to the passage of the historic Waikato-Tainui Settlement, which included in the legislation a formal apology by the New Zealand Crown for how it dealt with the Māori. After granting Royal Assent to the legislation, Queen Elizabeth II (along with Prime Minister Jim Bolger) signed a written letter of apology to the Tainui people at Wellington's Government House witnessed by the Māori Queen and other dignitaries.[4]

In Canada, discussions around integrating Indigenous aspects (in partnership with the relevant First Nations) within the day-to-day lives of the provincial Crowns could be coordinated during the annual vice-regal conferences, with the Dignified Crown/First Nations relationships fixed as a permanent feature of the agenda. Back in their home provinces, consistent policies and protocols could be developed by the lieutenant governors' offices in consultation with, and with the consent of, Indigenous communities. These protocols and relationships would transcend the individual lieutenant governor and become embedded in the very heart of the office itself. Such a development would have the added effect of addressing an issue that plagues the contemporary Dignified Crown in Canada: the lack of corporate memory.

A fundamental contradiction exists with the Dignified Crown of Canada in that while one of constitutional monarchy's greatest advantages is the perception of continuity, the reality is that there is little institutional memory in the offices of the Queen's representatives in Canada. Speaking to the Department of Aboriginal Studies at the University of Toronto in 2014, Alan Corbiere highlighted this problem in his discussion "Living Treaty and the Necessity of Corporate Memory":

> What ends up happening is people that end up succeeding in the role of deputy superintendent, or superintendent general of Indian Affairs, or lieutenant governor, they don't get apprised of the responsibilities. They have a total lack of knowledge of treaties that have been passed down as well as the diplomatic nature of the discourse when they meet in council..… Now [they all] look at it in a legalistic framework.…[5]

For many vice-regal offices across the country, the incoming official representative directs what themes will be supported and ceremonies attended. In many ways, the Dignified Canadian Crown resets itself with every appointment of a lieutenant governor or governor general. This continual resetting contrasts sharply with the radically different approach to time and history taken by Indigenous cultures and has often resulted in conflicts. To improve relations between the Dignified Crown and Indigenous peoples, the lack of institutional memory in regards to First Nations relationships must be remedied.

Facilitating the renewal and polishing of the Covenant Chain must become one of the official and publicized duties of the representatives of the Crown in Canada — this cannot be left to the chance that such acts will fall within identified themes articulated by individual vice-regal offices and representatives.[6] Explicit definition needs to be made within every vice-regal office that formalizes the governors general and lieutenant governors as representatives/keepers of the Treaty relationship. Currently, the most important job of vice-regal officials in this country is articulated as ensuring that Canada and its provinces always have first ministers at the heads of their governments. This should be amended to include a reference to their role as the official representative of the Queen's personal relationship with Indigenous peoples.[7] In the *2013 Annual Statement of the Lieutenant Governor of British Columbia*, one of the vice-regal roles is explained as "perpetu[ating] the traditional bond between the Crown and First Nations."[8] Adding a reference to a personal (familial) relationship, such a statement (explaining the vice-regal role of tending the fire, receiving and presenting gifts, et cetera) could be entrenched in the publicly stated duties of the vice-regal representatives across the country.

"The monarchy has been grappling with its role since Charles II [the Restoration of 1660]," Steven Point noted to me in an interview, "… [and in Canada] vice-regals need to understand that their constitutional roles are bigger and broader than simply being window dressing."

Explaining the role of lieutenant governor in Canada, Point says, "… the lieutenant governors hold sovereignty on behalf of the Queen, and they need to understand this in light of their roles with First Nations and learn how it interfaces with them … lieutenant governors have a historic obligation to look out for the best interests of First Nations." When asked about the political implications of such a statement, Point laughs, "You can't take the politics out of the Sovereign!"[9]

Each vice-regal office could develop clearly defined and distinct (depending on the Nation involved) policies around advising the official representatives of Her Majesty on the Treaty relationships and protocols they entail. Key areas could be developed that affirm the personal bond with the Monarch, highlighting the respect and equality that such a relationship entails. Such advice would naturally be the responsibility of the private secretary or chief of staff, empowering Canada's vice-regal representatives and strengthening their offices while at the same time avoiding embarrassing missteps in their constitutional roles. Private secretaries should begin the process of educating their respective lieutenant governors or governors general about their Treaty obligations once their appointment has been announced, a process that should include formal and informal meetings with Indigenous leaders, constitutional experts, and other relevant figures.

### Keeper of the Queen's Fire

The Dignified Crown has the unique ability to rekindle the council fires (official places where treaties are negotiated, conflicts handled, and relationships fostered in the northeast of the continent[10]) like the one lit by Sir William Johnson at Niagara.

An important part of the Covenant Chain relationship, fires are places to gather and sit in community, talking through the various ups and downs that different worldviews naturally create. I would suggest fixing the main fire at Rideau Hall (the Queen's Canadian residence), with subsidiary fires at the various provincial Government Houses (and in the unfortunate cases of Quebec and Ontario, which have lost their official residences, at their vice-regal offices). While the Dignified Crown, restricted by responsible government and constitutional monarchy, cannot be a direct participant in negotiations and conflict resolution, it retains the equally important task of providing an apolitical and respectful space in which Treaty can be fostered and renewed. Indeed, the official representatives of the Crown evoke the "Honour of the Crown" that is key to the Treaty relationship.

It is important to emphasize that the "Queen's Fire" kept at Rideau Hall and the provincial Government Houses only represents part of the Treaty relationship. Wherever First Nations fix their council fires (or other mediums of Treaty) must be honoured by the Crown and treated with the same respect as those fixed at the vice-regal homes. Protocols will need to be developed for the vice-regal fires (What happens when a delegation arrives at a fire? Who is there to greet them? How is access to the lieutenant governor or governor general assured?) as well as for when the Crown is asked to attend a council/meeting (as Chief Theresa Spence requested in 2012–2013).

Given the diversity and individual histories, it would be naive to say that the Queen's Fire would have the same significance from sea to sea to sea. Council fires (and tools such as wampum and pipes) as diplomatic mediums have little meaning to the Métis, Inuit, and Indigenous peoples of the West Coast and British Columbian interior. While seeing fire as a place of gathering is virtually universal, its formalization into a diplomatic space is largely relegated to the eastern and central regions of the continent. Each vice-regal office would have to adapt its manifestation of the Queen's Fire to meet the needs of the protocols required by its

Governor General Michaëlle Jean joins in an Inuit feast that included eating raw seal meat during a 2009 visit to Rankin Inlet, Nunavut. Jean's participation was widely seen within the Inuit community as an act of respect. © *The Queen in Right of Canada represented by the Office of the Secretary to the Governor General (2009). Sgt. Serge Gouin, Rideau Hall. Reproduced with permission of the Office of the Secretary to the Governor General.*

specific relationships. There may even be instances where a fire as a gathering place would be inappropriate — flexibility and open communication between Treaty partners is key to navigating these discussions.

## Access to the Queen and Her Official Representatives

Royal and vice-regal events and tours must include meaningful opportunities to meet with Indigenous peoples. Tours should include time with First Nations' leadership (both hereditary and elected) on their territory to allow for formal exchanges of gifts, greetings, and the presentation of petitions.

For example, if a Royal Tour is to be conducted in Fredericton, then a meeting should happen with Mi'kmaq and Maliseet leaders at a place of their choosing (not in a line on an airport tarmac). If these meetings are taking place, they should be publicized with a strong emphasis on educating the public on their significance and importance to treaty relationships. As I have said before, the work of the Earl and Countess of Wessex in this country should be seen as a model of how all Royal and vice-regal tours should be conducted.

Of course, what often gets in the way of such interactions is that the Dignified Crown in this country must follow the advice of its elected ministers. If the Government of Canada advises the Queen or her official representatives not to meet with Indigenous leadership, they are bound to follow this advice (sadly, there is a long tradition of such advice). This is why, in the interests of reconciliation, such advice must no longer be offered. The special and personal Treaty relationships must be honoured. Access to the Dignified Crown does not violate responsible government, although it may get uncomfortable at times owing to the grievances that may be aired. Non-Indigenous Canadians can no longer have a monopoly over the Dignified Crown in this country.

## Receiving Petitions

In September 2013, First Nation parties to Ontario's Robinson-Huron Treaty served a notice of claim concerning outstanding annuities and a violation of Treaty to the offices of both the governor general and the lieutenant governor of Ontario.[11] Due to the strictures of responsible government, the federal and provincial representatives of the Canadian Crown were required to forward these notices to the appropriate government organs.

The passage of these petitions and notices from the Dignified Crown to the relevant government department is an important act: the Crown acts as the guarantor that the message from the people it is bound to will be safely delivered to the appropriate destinations. Such an act goes beyond the symbolic, even though it has become automatic, because it directly evokes the "Honour of the Crown." As explained in the Final Report of the 1996 Royal Commission on Aboriginal Peoples, the

One of the medallions distributed during the 1977 commemorations of the one-hundredth anniversary of the conclusion of Treaty Seven attended by the Prince of Wales. One side of the medallion depicts the original Treaty Seven medal given to the chiefs in 1877, while the other depicts the crown worn by Prince Charles at his investiture as Prince of Wales in 1969. *Courtesy of author.*

concept of the Canadian Crown is seen "… as the protector of the sovereignty of Aboriginal peoples within Canada and as guarantor of their Aboriginal and treaty rights."[12] The very act of receiving and transmitting messages from Indigenous peoples to the Government of Canada reinforces the Dignified Crown as a conduit for communication that infuses honour into the proceedings — it reminds the Government of Canada of its fiduciary obligations as the actor behind the country's constitutional monarchy.

As explained earlier, the act of petitioning the Queen has deep roots in this country that stretch all the way to the very beginnings of the Covenant Chain relationship. The Monarch as a figure separate from the government is intrinsic to this relationship — an interpretation that is entirely correct in our modern constitutional monarchy (it is the interaction between the Dignified and Efficient Crowns that causes confusion between Indigenous and non-Indigenous peoples).

## Gift-Giving

The importance of gift-giving cannot be overstated. The act of giving a gift emphasizes equality and respect between the two parties. A regular feature between heads of state across the planet, the symbolism attached to these exchanges demonstrates to First Nations that they stand side-by-side with Canada (the Crown) as partners. Royal and vice-regal tours across this country need to include meetings with the Indigenous leadership (both traditional and elected) of the territories visited, as well as an exchange of gifts between the highest members in their respective orders of precedence. Just as when a foreign head of state visits Canada and stops, first, to pay a visit and exchange gifts with the governor general, so, too, must the same protocol be observed with visits to First Nations and/or with Indigenous peoples.

Left to right: Grand Council Chief Pat Madahbee, the Honourable David Zimmer, and Deputy Minister David de Launay of Ontario's Ministry of Aboriginal Affairs sit around the King's Fire during the commemorations of the 250th anniversary of the Treaty of Niagara, August 2, 2014. *Courtesy of author.*

During the commemorations of the 250th anniversary of the Treaty of Niagara at The Commons of Niagara-on-the-Lake, a powerful exchange of gifts occurred between the Government of Ontario and the representatives of the original twenty-four nations that ratified the Treaty in 1764. Witnessing the lighting of the King's Fire at sunrise on August 2 were Minister of Aboriginal Affairs David Zimmer and his deputy minister, David de Launay.

The two men sat on a mat (the traditional symbol of a Nation) around the fire. With the other nations present, they smoked the Unity Pipe given to Grand Council Chief Pat Madahbee, addressing the assembly at different times, and participating in constructive conversations around the Crown/First Nation relationship. It was during the formal addresses that Minister Zimmer, on behalf of Premier Kathleen Wynne and her Cabinet, presented a beautiful and symbolic gift to the twenty-four nations.

Zimmer said:

In honour of the Treaty of Niagara of 1764, and on behalf of the Crown, I would like to offer a gift to each of the twenty-four Indigenous Nations that were present at the time of the treaty ratification process. The gifting of the wampum strings is a symbolic gesture that is meant to renew the relationships affirmed by the Treaty of Niagara. This gift contains two strings of wampum, in which one string represents the Indigenous Nation and the second string represents the Crown. By extending this gift, it is an important reminder of our responsibility to uphold the honour of the Crown and further symbolizes the rekindling of the King's Fire.[13]

The representatives of the original twenty-four nations at the Great Council of Niagara stand with Ontario's minister of aboriginal affairs after exchanging gifts on August 2, 2014. The First Nations delegates hold their strings of wampum while the minister displays a replica of the Friendship Wampum. *Courtesy of author.*

This was clearly a gift that had been thought out, invoking both the Covenant Chain Wampum and the *Teioháte Kaswenta*. Thanking Ontario for the gift, Rick Hill (representing the Six Nations Legacy Consortium) presented Minister Zimmer with a replica of the Friendship Wampum.

The only downside to this event was that the lieutenant governor was not the one presenting the gift on behalf of *his* government. The presence of the Dignified Crown would have elevated the meeting from simply a government-of-the-day meeting to that of one that was truly nation-to-nation (here I am defining Ontario as a nation).

Similar ceremonies could be devised for a multitude of occasions across the country. Acts, such as the first meeting between a specific First Nation and a governor general, or lieutenant governor, could be modelled on the ceremonies surrounding the arrival of ambassadors and high commissioners at Rideau Hall to present their credentials, or consulates

Ken Maracle accepts two strings of wampum from Minister Zimmer on behalf of the Cayuga Nation. *Courtesy of author.*

SUGGESTIONS FOR MOVING FORWARD TOGETHER

Queen Elizabeth II in her capacity as Queen of Canada stands with a member of the Royal Canadian Mounted Police before dedicating the cornerstone (which included a stone from Runnymede, site of the signing of the 1215 Magna Carta), of the Canadian Museum for Human Rights in Winnipeg, Manitoba, in 2010. The museum is located on The Forks, an important Indigenous meeting site at the confluence of the Red River and Assiniboine River. Earlier that year, Governor General Michaëlle Jean visited The Forks to attend ceremonies for the Truth and Reconciliation Commission. © *Press Association.*

paying courtesy calls to the various provincial Government Houses (or offices). These public and regular exchanges of "presents" would be a powerful educational moment for Indigenous and non-Indigenous peoples across the country.

Gifts given by the Dignified Crown must have meaning and, if possible, include Royal and vice-regal emblems, as well as any symbols that reference the personal relationship between the Sovereign and Indigenous Nation (there are historic precedents of presenting special medals at important councils or other Treaty gatherings). It is important that these gifts come from the Queen and/or her official representatives directly, and, so, underscore the personal nature of the relationship that is being renewed.

## Indigenous Recognition of the Canadian Crown

There remains an "elephant in the room" when discussing First Nations and the Dignified Crown in this country. In his recent book *The Crown and Canadian Federalism*, Dr. D. Michael Jackson highlights the 1996 Royal Commission on Aboriginal Peoples recommendation that First Nations form a third order of government in Canada's unique federation. In fact, citing the Tsilhqot'in Nation, Peter Russell states that "… with respect to the management and development of land and resources …," Canada now has three orders of government (federal, provincial, and — where Aboriginal title is established — Indigenous).[14]

Citing the work of Poelzer and Coates as well as of that of David E. Smith, Jackson explains that the Canadian Crown has evolved into a compound monarchy. There is now "a divided Crown, federal and provincial, and … the provinces [are] led by their own powerful executives in possession of sovereignty in their own right…."[15] If the Canadian Crown is evolving to adapt to the realities of Indigenous sovereignty, this is another reminder that our constitutional monarchy is no longer solely within the purview of non-Indigenous Canadians to define. Perhaps the greatest stumbling block in developing a common definition of the Crown in Canada centres on the very DNA of the monarchy itself.

Dr. Jackson makes the point that our constitutional monarchy is no longer headed by the British Monarch; rather, it is the Queen of Canada that personifies the Canadian State. However, most Indigenous peoples, including their leadership, see their Treaty relationships with the British Crown and not its Canadian descendant. Numerous petitions by First Nations are sent to Queen Elizabeth II as the "Queen of England," or the British Monarch, reflecting the notion that the eighteenth-, nineteenth-, and early twentieth-century treaties made expressly between Indigenous peoples and the Crown in Britain remain as such in the twenty-first century. In many ways, the Indigenous interpretation of

Canada's constitutional monarchy remains pre-Statute of Westminster in nature — there remains a belief that the British Monarch still has the power to intervene when Canadian governments stray from the agreements that were made.

For Canadians, such an arrangement has not been a constitutional reality since the 1931 Statute of Westminster set in motion developments leading to a distinct Canadian monarchy, albeit one that shares the same Monarch as the British (as well as fourteen other Commonwealth realms). In this country, Queen Elizabeth II is the Queen of Canada, the embodiment of the Canadian State since ascending the throne in 1952. The Queen's official representatives in this country represent her as the Queen of Canada, with no constitutional links to Elizabeth II as Sovereign of the United Kingdom.

This political reality was emphasized, in Britain no less, during the turbulent constitutional discussions of early 1980s when the Indian Association of Alberta, the Union of New Brunswick Indians, and the Union of Nova Scotia Indians appealed to the High Court of Justice in England to intercede on their behalf and stop the Trudeau government's effort to transfer the amending formula for the Constitution to the Canadian Parliament. Ultimately, Lord Denning, of the English Court of Appeal, ruled that it was the Canadian Crown and not the British Crown that was responsible for the Treaty relationship. In his book, Dr. Jackson quotes Lord Justice Kerr as saying, "… rights and obligations in relation to the Indian peoples are therefore the responsibility of the Crown in Right of *the Dominion or Provinces of Canada* [Jackson deliberately emphasizes this reference to a compound monarchy], not the Crown in Right of the United Kingdom."[16] Indeed, if Canada is to further compound its constitutional monarchy by adding another order of government, Indigenous peoples and their Nations must recognize on their own terms that Elizabeth II, as Queen of Canada, is the inheritor of their Treaty relationships.

This understanding does not, in any way, detract from the fact that Indigenous peoples remain bound to the Queen and her family. In fact, the remarkable versatility of Canada's constitutional monarchy allows it to claim the British Royal Family as its own. Emphasizing that the Royal Family is also a distinctly Canadian institution, something most non-Indigenous Canadians have lost touch with, allows for a much smoother transfer of the Treaty relationship. Rather than being seen as a colonial holdover, the fact that Elizabeth II, the British Monarch, is also Elizabeth II, the Queen of Canada, should be embraced. If the Treaty relationship is to be honoured, the DNA of the Crown has to be acknowledged by both sides: Canadians must remember that the 1931 Statute of Westminster did not abrogate the personal Treaty relationship established by the British Crown, and Indigenous peoples must see the Dignified Canadian Crown as the natural inheritor of the Covenant Chain relationship.

With all of this being said, it is important to emphasize that Indigenous peoples are being asked to embrace a Canadian Crown even though the creation and evolution of the country's constitutional monarchy was done without their initial consultation or consent.

Poelzer and Coates's *Aboriginal Peoples and the Crown in Canada: Completing the Canadian Experiment* highlights another area where some sort of agreement must be reached between the First Nations and Canada. While Poelzer and Coates agree, "A third order of government … is consistent with the historical and institutional foundations of Canada,"[17] they recognize that First Nations see their treaty relationship with only the federal government. The emergence of the provincial governments as sovereign entities, and lieutenant governors as distinct representatives of the Crown in their own rights, has evolved over the past century and a half since Confederation without consultation with Indigenous peoples.

It is ironic that most of the work of reconciliation being done by the Dignified Crown in this country is by its lieutenant governors, officers that represent political entities that do not have Treaty relationships with First Nations. While Canada's compound monarchy is a vehicle to politically reconcile the relationship between First Nations and the State, this can only be done if the nation-to-nation relationship is expanded to include the provinces (which now see themselves as co-sovereign with the federal government). The divisibility of the Canadian Crown has to be acknowledged and divorced from the unitary nature that the British Crown historically provided.

There is a region of the country that recognizes and affirms the compound nature of the Canadian Crown. Established in 1992, the British Columbia Treaty Commission exists to facilitate "treaty negotiations among the governments of Canada, B.C., and First Nations in B.C."[18] The commission's six-stage process allows the three parties to negotiate both "agreements in principle," as well as modern treaties (apart from the Douglas Treaties on Vancouver Island and Treaty Eight, no treaties were concluded between the Crown and First Nations now within British Columbia). This process acknowledges the legal separation of the Queen into her national and provincial manifestations, with all "agreements in principle" and treaties defining the Crown as meaning "Her Majesty the Queen in Right of Canada or Her Majesty the Queen in Right of British Columbia, as the case may be." While "Her Majesty the Queen in Right of Canada" is a legal definition meaning the federal state, it does suggest the establishment of a relationship. As well, the inclusion of the "Queen in Right of British Columbia" creates an official relationship with the lieutenant governor as Her Majesty's official provincial representative.

The landmark 1999 Nisga'a Final Agreement between Canada, British Columbia, and the Nisga'a expressly defines the province as "Her Majesty the Queen in Right of British Columbia" and the country as "Her Majesty the Queen in Right of Canada" and is signed separately by representatives on her behalf.

We must, to quote the Prince of Wales (speaking in 2014 about the strength of Canada to CBC interviewer George Stroumboulopoulos), see the Crown as creating unity from its diversity (or one state from its many distinct, and equal, compound elements). If we are to complete the Canadian experiment, the provincial components of the Crown need to be recognized before an Indigenous dimension can be established.

An interesting question does arise in that if a true third order of government is to be created in this country, will Canada's constitutional monarchy require a new official representative of the Dignified Crown for the First Nations to reflect the political reality of a federal, provincial, and now Indigenous dimension of the Crown? For such an office to be truly effective, its appointment must come from the Queen (in consultation with Indigenous leadership). Such a change to the Constitution would also provide the opportunity to elevate the office of lieutenant governor to being a true equal to the governor general (having appointments come directly from the Sovereign, and accorded the same protocols and dignities). While the title associated with this new vice-regal office should be determined in consultation with Indigenous peoples, I would offer "Commissioner" as a starting point (to avoid confusion, the territories would need to have lieutenant governors appointed to them — a natural political evolution that is already in motion).

### Separating Canada's Efficient and Dignified Crowns in the Minds of Indigenous Peoples and Non-Indigenous Canadians

For non-Indigenous Canadians, a different task presents itself. The feeling of an active, direct relationship with the Sovereign has been divorced from the experience of mainstream Canadian society (arguably, such a relationship has never existed in North America between a subject/citizen and the Monarch). For Canadians, while laws may be enforced, justice delivered, and government performed in the name of the Queen, the idea of the Monarch having an active role in government would be intolerable. For non-Indigenous Canadians, the Dignified Crown is largely at arms' length due to the fact that Queen Elizabeth II does not reside on this side of the Atlantic (and is also shared amongst fifteen other realms) and the fact that real political power is exercised in her name by elected officials.

The closest most Canadians get to their Monarch is through interactions with her official representatives: the governor general and lieutenant governors. As points of contact, these officials "Canadianize" the institution, personalizing it according to the different jurisdictions of Canada, while at the same time infusing the Crown with their own interests and focuses. Still, despite the personal touches provided by the vice-regal representatives to their jurisdictions, Queen Elizabeth II herself remains an often-evoked, yet distant entity. The reality of responsible government and the exercise of the Crown's prerogatives by elected officials have led to most Canadians dismissing the role of the Dignified Crown as being no more than "symbolic." Such a word, coupled with such phrases as "a link to our history," relegate the Dignified Crown to nothing more than a historic curiosity in the minds of the general public.

Conversely, time and time again Indigenous peoples seem to portray the Dignified Crown as still having the powers of the Efficient Crown. The line between the Queen and her Canadian government is often blurred for First Nations, even though it crystallized centuries ago for her non-Indigenous subjects.

Walter Bagehot's definition of a modern constitutional monarchy has been accepted into Canada's unwritten constitution without consultation or agreement by the Queen's Indigenous allies and partners. Perhaps this last line captures the whole problem. However, the question remains: What can be done to move forward?

The Crown in Canada (and the United Kingdom) has changed, fracturing into Dignified and Efficient dimensions. In order to move forward, First Nations must agree that this political reality exists when dealing with Canada, and that the Queen and her representatives cannot intervene in the constitutional governing by their elected representatives.

Saying that, it is equally important that non-Indigenous Canadians stop ignoring the tremendously important roles that the Dignified Crown plays in this country, as well as the relationships it still is required to honour and uphold. Freed from the often toxic political arena, the Queen and her representatives retain the extraordinary ability to build community and facilitate the direct access of Indigenous peoples and their leadership to the government of the day. Regarding the interaction of Indigenous peoples with Canada, the Dignified Crown in this country retains the duty (I would say, sacred duty) to inform the Efficient Crown with respect to the Treaty relationships across the land.

Commenting on the Ontario Court of Appeal's 2014 upholding of the Canadian Oath to the Queen against a constitutional challenge by three permanent residents, University of Ottawa Professor of Political Science Philippe Lagassé wrote, "… the judgment found that the meaning of the 'Queen of Canada' has evolved to represent Canadian democracy and the institutions of Canadian government." Lagassé warns that such an abstract definition could be dangerous for the institution:

> In stating that the oath is to the Queen of Canada as a symbol of government and not to Queen Elizabeth II as a natural person, both [Justice] Weiler and [Justice] Morgan are implying that the office of the Queen and the holder of that office, Queen Elizabeth II, can be disaggregated.[19]

For non-Indigenous Canadians, a scenario is emerging that could see a Canadian Crown that no longer needs a Monarch to exist. Canadians need to turn to their Indigenous brothers and sisters and learn from them, rediscovering the Dignified Crown, and the important role in our collective society that it fulfills.

That treaties are explicitly made with the Monarch is key to understanding the relationships they have established. Employing Indigenous diplomatic language, treaty negotiators gave the impression of an active, benevolent Monarch who was in direct, personal relationship with First Nations, even though the evolution of the British Constitution (and the idea of responsible government) made such a thing impossible. By articulating Queen Victoria as "Mother," treaty negotiators thought they were simply using terms that their Indigenous counterparts would understand, whereas, in reality, they were fusing the Dignified and Efficient Crowns, establishing relationships that their political system was incapable of realizing. However, that fact remains that it was done, and now Canadians must respect those relationships (that have become constitutionally enshrined thanks to the Canadian Charter of Rights and Freedoms).

Beyond the treaties, Canadians would do well to see the extraordinary (and unique) role the Dignified Crown has in this country, celebrating, unifying, and stabilizing society. In a country as diverse and varied as Canada, the very survival of this Confederation is due in no small part to the Dignified Crown, at times despite the best efforts of its "Efficient" alter-ego.

## A New Great Council and Renewed Treaties

The 1764 Council of Niagara could serve as a model to reconcile and reaffirm the personal relationship with Elizabeth II as Queen of Canada, as well as her representatives, while at the same time educating Canadians about this very important bond. Using wampum and other traditional Indigenous diplomatic methods, Indigenous peoples could be invited to recognize a renewed relationship with Queen Elizabeth II (the great-great granddaughter of Queen Victoria), now as the embodiment of the Canadian Crown. The restoration of such important acts as gift-giving, petitioning, and so forth would provide an opportunity to define the Dignified Crown's role in Canada, and bind the Queen of Canada in a renewed (or re-polished) Covenant. The 150th anniversary of Confederation, whose original celebration did not include Indigenous peoples, provides an excellent opportunity to begin this process by calling for a new Great Council.

Protocols would need to be developed and negotiated in a respectful and meaningful way. The council would need to be co-chaired by the Queen and Indigenous leadership (both traditional and elected), with the ultimate goal of bringing all the "Treaty Peoples" (Indigenous and non-Indigenous) into relationship with one another. While the Dignified Crown no longer has the ability to negotiate on behalf of the Canadian public, it remains as an active conduit for respectful and meaningful communication. In its capacity to advise, the Dignified Crown would ensure that the honour of the Crown was being upheld, and that the elected government was fully accessible to its Indigenous partners. Far from being just symbolic, such a role would be both active and deeply relevant to the path of reconciliation.

The fact that the Treaty of Niagara exists proves that we once understood one another — non-Indigenous and Indigenous peoples of this land once existed in relationship with each other. Since those earlier days, the settler population has strayed into the Indigenous path, imposing laws and world views that run contrary to their realities. If we are to polish the Covenant Chain, removing ourselves from their vessel and returning to our own, the Dignified Crown will have to be involved (as in many ways it already is). In doing so, we must accept that this process could take generations, but realize and take comfort in the fact that our journey toward reconciliation becomes the new Treaty itself.

# Notes

## Introduction

1. Tsilhqot'in Nation v. British Columbia, [2014] SCC 44.
2. Peter Russell, "Tsilhqot'in Nation v. British Columbia: Can the Successful Defence of Aboriginal Title in Courts Pave the Way to Reconciliation?," University of Toronto, 2014.
3. David E. Smith, *The Invisible Crown: The First Principle of Canadian Government* (Toronto: University of Toronto Press, 1995), x.
4. It meant so much to have Reilly McCleary, Alex Hughes, Miles Evans Branagh, Mike Evans Branagh, Dody Evans, and Terry Branagh present at the completion of the wampum on March 8, 2014.
5. The traditional homelands of the Haudenosaunee Confederacy are south and southeast of Lake Ontario. Allied to the British Crown during the American War for Independence (1775–1783), some of the Haudenosaunee moved north after the creation of the American Republic, settling along land granted to them.
6. Most replicas are made using glass beads instead of the tradition quahog shell beads due to their cost (to recreate the 1764 Covenant Chain Wampum in quahog beads would have cost around $50,000.00 CDN).
7. Treaty Canoe is a performance/sculpture/installation by Alex MacKay made from cedar, copper wire, birchbark, red-ribbon, glue, and treaties hand-penned onto hand-made linen paper. Treaty Canoe speaks of mutual bonds of honour, making it clear that we are all treaty people. Created in 1999, Treaty Canoe and its sister piece Treaty of Niagara 1764 have been displayed at such locations as the Canadian Canoe Museum, the University of Kent (UK) and the Indigenous Bar Association's commemoration of the Royal Proclamation at Rama First Nation.
8. The Committee's members were Holly McCann (cartographer), Kekoa Reinebold (Brown Cabin Researcher), Ishkwegiizhig (Eugene Kahgee of the Saugeen First Nation #29), Councillor Judi Partridge (Ward 15 Flamborough) and Nathan Tidridge (Chair). Elder Garry Sault of the Mississaugas of

the New Credit First Nation consulted with the committee, providing invaluable teachings.
9. Nathan Tidridge, "Waterdown Natural Area Report to the City of Hamilton," May 30, 2014.
10. Chief M. Bryan Laforme of the Mississaugas of the New Credit First Nation, Dedication of the Souharissen Natural Area, August 21, 2014. Chief Laforme also remarked "This is an important event for our Nation. The 104 archeological sites discovered here prove that at one time a flourishing Anishinaabe culture existed all along the shores of these Great Lakes. These lakes and rivers fed and sustained us and provided vital transportation routes that allowed for trade. This truly is our homeland and returning home is always a good feeling. It must be remembered, however, that First Nation concepts of land differ from those of the modern world. We view ourselves not as individual owners but instead as collective caretakers. These lands belong to children yet unborn. Our job is to preserve it for future generations. We invite you to be partners in this mission."
11. The first elected female chief of the Mississaugas of the New Credit First Nation.

## Chapter One: Encountering Indigenous Voices

1. This canoe became the centrepiece of a garden created with Carolyn King of the Mississaugas of the New Credit in June 2015 to celebrate the PanAm Games being held in Toronto (on the Mississaugas traditional territory) that year. The garden is located within Waterdown's Souharissen Natural Area.
2. Nathan Tidridge, *Beyond Mainland*, (Carlisle: St*one Soup Publications, 2009), 14.
3. Numerous references to Canada's residential school program can be found woven into the different curricula across the country. Interestingly, the new 2013 Ontario Grade 7 Social Studies Curriculum includes a direct reference to the Treaty of Niagara in its specific expectation A3.2: "Identify key political and legal changes that occurred in, and/or affected Canada during [1713–1800]. Eg. The Treaty of Utrecht, the Treaties of Peace and Friendship, The Royal Proclamation of 1763, the Niagara Treaty of 1764 . . .," *The Ontario Curriculum: Social Studies, Grades 1-6, History and Geography, Grade 7-8* (Toronto: Ministry of Education, 2013), 140.

# NOTES

4. The institute was first announced by John Fraser, Fourth Master of Massey College, in the presence of the Right Honourable David Johnston, governor general of Canada, and the Honourable David Onley, lieutenant governor of Ontario, during the launch of *Canada and the Crown* (McGill-Queen's University Press, 2014) at Queen's Park. Fraser explained that one of the Institute's goals was to "... organize alliances, organizations or simple liaison status ... with First Nation treaty organizations." February 12, 2014.
5. Hosted by the Province of Saskatchewan and the Johnson-Shoyama Graduate School of Public Policy at the University of Saskatchewan and University of Regina from October 26–28, 2012.
6. J.R. (Jim) Miller, "The Aboriginal Peoples and the Crown," in *Canada and the Crown: Essays in Constitutional Monarchy*, ed. D. Michael Jackson and Philippe Lagassé (Montreal & Kingston: McGill-Queen's University Press, 2013), 256.
7. John Borrows, "Fragile Freedoms: Indigenous Love, Law and Land in Canada's Constitution," *Ideas with Paul Kennedy*, CBC, March 5, 2014.
8. Justice Murray Sinclair, Address, British Columbia Reconciliation Week, September 16, 2013.
9. http://english.stackexchange.com/questions/55486/what-are-the-percentages-of-the-parts-of-speech-in-english.
10. Bruce Morito, *An Ethic of Mutual Respect: The Covenant Chain and Aboriginal-Crown Relations* (Toronto: UBC Press, 2012), 7.
11. Professor Bruce Morito to Nathan Tidridge, email, May 1, 2014.
12. Gregory Evans Dowd, *War Under Heaven* (Baltimore: The Johns Hopkins University Press, 2002), 9.
13. Ibid, 11.
14. Sarah Carter, "'Your Great Mother Across the Salt Sea': Prairie First Nations, the British Monarchy and the Vice Regal Connection to 1900," *Manitoba History* 48, (Autumn/Winter 2004–5). www.mhs.mb.ca/docs/mb_history/48/greatmother.shtml.
15. Ibid.
16. Alexander Morris, *The Treaties of Canada with the Indians of Manitoba and the North-West Territories* (Toronto: Coles Publishing, 1971), 199–200.
17. Ibid, 200.
18. Ibid, 296–97.
19. Sarah Carter, "'Your Great Mother Across the Salt Sea': Prairie First Nations, the British Monarchy and the Vice Regal Connection to 1900."

20. Peter Carstens, *The Queen's People: A Study of Hegemony, Coercion, and Accommodation among the Okanagan of Canada* (Toronto: University of Toronto Press, 1991), xv.
21. Bruce Morito, *An Ethic of Mutual Respect: The Covenant Chain and Aboriginal-Crown Relations* (Vancouver: UBC Press, 2012), 73.
22. Royal Commission on Aboriginal Peoples, *Part One: The Relationship in Historical Perspective*, (Ottawa, Royal Commission on Aboriginal Peoples, 1996), 36.
23. Daniel K. Richter, "Indian-Colonist Conflicts and Alliances," in *Encyclopedia of the North American Colonies*, ed. Jacob Ernest Cooke (New York: Charles Scribner's Sons, 1993), 223–36.
24. *Legacy of Hope and Healing* (Ottawa: Legacy of Hope Foundation, 2011), 1.
25. Thomas King, *The Truth About Stories* (Toronto: Anansi, 2003), 9–10.
26. Eva MacKay, "The Apologizers' Apology," in *Reconciling Canada: Critical Perspectives on the Culture of Redress*, ed. Jennifer Henderson and Pauline Wakeham (Toronto: University of Toronto Press, 2013), 49.
27. Gregory Evans Dowd, *War Under Heaven*, 64.
28. Genocide is defined in Article 2 of the Convention on the Prevention and Punishment of the Crime of Genocide (1948) as "any of the following acts committed with intent to destroy, in whole or in part, a national, ethnical, racial or religious group, as such: killing members of the group; causing serious bodily or mental harm to members of the group; deliberately inflicting on the group conditions of life calculated to bring about its physical destruction in whole or in part; imposing measures intended to prevent births within the group; [and] forcibly transferring children of the group to another group."
29. Stephen Lewis, "A Socialist Takes Stock," Symons Lecture, Charlottetown, Prince Edward Island, November 21, 2014.

### Chapter Two: The 1764 Treaty of Niagara and Covenant Chain of Friendship

1. Milton W. Hamilton, *The Papers of Sir William Johnson*, vol. XI (Albany: University of the State of New York, 1953), 309.
2. J. R. Miller, *Compact, Contract, Covenant: Aboriginal Treaty-Making in*

# NOTES

      *Canada* (Toronto: University of Toronto Press, 2009), 41.

3. In *Anishinaabewin Niiwin: Four Rising Winds* (2013), ed. Alan Ojiig Corbiere, Mary Ann Naokwegijig Corbiere, Deborah McGregor, and Crystal Migwans (M'Chigeeng, ON: Ojibwe Cultural Foundation, 2014).
4. Leslie MacKinnon, "Royal Proclamation of 1763, Canada's 'Indian Magna Carta,' turns 250: A pivotal moment in Canadian and First Nations history gets a small celebration," *CBC News*, www.cbc.ca, October 6, 2013.
5. Justice Murray Sinclair, Commemoration of the Royal Proclamation, Chippewa of Rama First Nation, October 7, 2013.
6. John Borrows, "Constitutional Principles Regulating Interaction Between First Nations and the Crown", Ph. D. diss., University of Toronto. 1994, 84.
7. James Sullivan, ed., *The Papers of William Johnson*, vol. III (Albany: New York University State Press, 1962), 457.
8. Gregory Evans Dowd, *War Under Heaven*, 64.
9. Ibid, 72.
10. Ibid, 126.
11. John Borrows, "Wampum at Niagara: The Royal Proclamation, Canadian Legal History, and Self Government," in *Aboriginal and Treaty Rights in Canada*, ed. Michael Asch (Vancouver: UBC Press, 1997), 162.
12. C. Flick, ed. *The Papers of Sir William Johnson*, vol. IV (Albany: University of the State of New York, 1925), 328–33.
13. Ibid, 332.
14. Ibid, 333.
15. John Borrows, "Constitutional Principals Regulating Interaction between First Nations and the Crown," 57.
16. During the commemorations of the 250th anniversary of the Treaty of Niagara the following list of participants at the 1764 Council, compiled by Six Nations' lawyer Paul Williams, was circulated: (The Six Nation Confederacy) Mohawks, Oneidaes, Tuscaroras, Onondagaes, Cayugaes, Senecas, Coghnawageys, Ganughsadageys, Nanticokes, Canoys, Mohicanders, Algonkins and Nipissengs; (The Western Confederacy) Chippawaes, Ottawaes, Menomineys, Sakis, Outagamies, Puans, Christineaux, Hurons, Toughkamiwons, [Algonkins], and [Nipissings].
17. John Borrows, "Constitutional Principals Regulating Interaction between First Nations and the Crown," 59. It is likely that there were members of the

Mi'kmaq and Dakota Nations (either as individuals or representatives of their respective nations) present at the Council of Niagara, even though there are no textual references to support this. However, oral history, historical context and the scholarship of Paul Williams ("The Chain," Master's Thesis, Osgoode Hall Law School, 1982) and John Borrows provide evidence of the attendance of the Dakota and Mi'kmaq (either as national representatives, traders, husbands/wives, etc.).

18. Rick Hill, "1764 Treaty of Fort Niagara Wampum Belts" (speech, Fort Niagara, 2014).
19. Milton W. Hamilton, *The Papers of Sir William Johnson*, vol. XI, 309.
20. Jamie Jacobs, *From Shells to Words*, Six Nations of the Grand River, April 30, 2014.
21. LAC, RG 10, reel C-1221, June 23, 1755, 28–53, quoted in Bruce Morito, *An Ethic of Mutual Respect: The Covenant Chain and Aboriginal-Crown Relations*, 24–25.
22. Bruce Morito, *An Ethic of Mutual Respect: The Covenant Chain and Aboriginal-Crown Relations*, 19.
23. Interestingly, the Throne Speech of British Columbia begins with the lieutenant governor recognizing prominent Indigenous and non-Indigenous people that have died since the previous opening of the legislature.
24. Alan Corbiere, "'Their own forms of which they take most notice': Diplomatic metaphors and symbolism on wampum belts," in *Anishinaabewin Niiwin: Four Rising Winds* (2013), 53.
25. The area between the upper and lower peninsulas of modern day Michigan.
26. Milton W. Hamilton, *The Papers of Sir William Johnson*, vol. XI, 311.
27. Alan Corbiere, "'Their own forms of which they take most notice': Diplomatic metaphors and symbolism on wampum belts," 53–55.
28. Translation by Rick Hill of Deyohahá:ge: Indigenous Knowledge Centre in Oshweken, Ontario.
29. Onondaga Nation: People of the Hills, www.onondaganation.org/culture/wpm_tworow.html, March 2, 2014.
30. Hayden King, "In thinking about what our country could become, we must be honest about our histories and include the perspectives of First Nations," *Toronto Star*, July 1, 2014, sec. A9.
31. Quoted in John Borrows, "Wampum at Niagara: The Royal Proclamation, Canadian Legal History, and Self Government," in *Aboriginal and Treaty Rights in Canada*, ed. Michael Asch (Vancouver: UBC Press, 1997), 170.

# NOTES

32. Bruce Morito, *An Ethic of Mutual Respect: The Covenant Chain and Aboriginal-Crown Relations,* 150.
33. Milton W. Hamilton, *The Papers of Sir William Johnson*, vol. XI, 394–96.
34. Ibid, 610.
35. Telephone conversation with the Honourable Steven L. Point, August 28, 2014.
36. *Reaffirming the Bond: The 2012 Royal Visit*, First Nations University, last modified September 14, 2014, www.fnuniv.ca/royalvisit.
37. Hamar Foster and Neil Vallance, *The Life and Times of the Royal Proclamation of 1763 in British Columbia,* activehistory.ca, October 3, 2013, http://activehistory.ca/2013/10/the-life-and-times-of-the-royal-proclamation-of-1763-in-british-columbia/.
38. Peter Russell gave a talk to the Arts & Letters Club of Toronto on February 25, 2014, about the Treaty of Niagara, entitled "Canada's First Confederation."
39. John Borrows, "Wampum at Niagara: The Royal Proclamation, Canadian Legal History, and Self Government," 169.
40. *Royal Proclamation of 1763: Relationships, Rights and Treaties*, Poster, Ministry of Aboriginal and Northern Affairs, 2013.
41. The Right Honourable David Johnston, Symposium in Honour of the 250th Anniversary of the Royal Proclamation, Gatineau, October 7, 2013.
42. Canadian Charter of Rights and Freedoms, s 2, Part I of the Constitution Act, 1982, being Schedule B to the Canada Act 1982 (UK), 1982, c 11.
43. Peter Carstens, *The Queen's People: A Study of Hegemony, Coercion, and Accommodation among the Okanagan of Canada* (Toronto: University of Toronto Press, 1991), xviii.

## Chapter Three: The Queen at the Council Fire

1. Peter Russell, "Understanding Canada: A Country Based on Incomplete Conquests," unpublished manuscript, 2014.
2. December 11, 2012–January 24, 2013.
3. Chief Theresa Spence, letter to His Excellency David Johnston, January 15, 2013.
4. His Excellency David Johnston, letter to Chief Theresa Spence, January 18, 2013.
5. Chief Theresa Spence, letter to His Excellency David Johnston, January 21, 2013.

6. Chief Theresa Spence, "Open letter to the national chief of the Assembly of First Nations, the Nishnawbe Aski Nation grand chief, and Ontario regional chief, Chiefs of Ontario," January 7, 2014.
7. Regional Chief Stan Beardy, "Urgent Open Letter to Her Majesty The Queen," December 20, 2012.
8. Justice Murray Sinclair, "Closing remarks to the Indigenous Bar Association," (speech, Orillia, ON, October 9, 2013).
9. *Nation to Nation: A resource on treaties in Ontario*, (North Bay: Union of Ontario Indians, 2013), 48.
10. Walter Bagehot, *The English Constitution* (London: Little, Brown, 1873), 85.
11. Honourable David C. Onley, "Witnessing Ceremony: Truth and Reconciliation Commission of Canada '2011 Circle of witness for the revitalizing reconciliation in Ontario: A cross-cultural dialogue,'" (speech, Toronto, September 28, 2011).
12. Prince Edward, Duke of Kent and Strathearn, "Letter to King George III," in *The Later Correspondance of George III*, vol. 1, ed. A. Aspinall (Cambridge: Cambridge University Press, 1962), 618.
13. Ian Radforth, *Royal Spectacle: The 1860 Visit of the Prince of Wales to Canada and the United States* (Toronto: University of Toronto Press, 2004), 230.
14. Peter Jones, *Life and Journals of Keh-ke-wa-guo-na-ba: (Rev. Peter Jones): Wesleyan Missionary* (Toronto: Anson Green, 1860), 338. In his journals, Keh-ke-wa-guo-na-ba notes a week prior to their audience with the King and Queen, the pair had visited Westminster Abbey, where they sat on the coronation chairs.
15. Ibid, 406–08.
16. ". . . Lord Glenelg introduced a Indian Chippewa Chief — who is [Christ]ian and come with a Petition. He is a tall, youngish man, with a yellowish complexion, and black hair; he was in National dress, which is entirely of leather; leather leggings; &c. He kissed my hand; he speaks English very well, and expressed himself very well." Queen Victoria, journal entry, September 14, 1838.
17. Elder Garry Sault, address at presentation of wampum to Lieutenant Governor David C. Onley and Premier Kathleen Wynne, Ontario Legislature, Toronto, June 24, 2014.
18. Richard Pennefather became famous during the 1860 Royal Tour when he fell out of the prince's steamer *Windsor* into the Detroit River and nearly drowned.

# NOTES

19. Quoted in Ian Radforth, *Royal Spectacle: The 1860 Visit of the Prince of Wales to Canada and the United States*, 232.
20. Quoted in J.R. (Jim) Miller, "The Aboriginal Peoples and the Crown," in *Canada and the Crown: Essays in Constitutional Monarchy*, ed. D. Michael Jackson and Philippe Lagassé (Montreal & Kingston: McGill-Queen's University Press, 2013), 261–62.
21. Foresters, Bank of Montreal, Torys LLP, and Royal Bank of Canada, *Doctor Oronhyatekha: A Mohawk of National Historic Significance* (Desronto, ON: Dr. Oronhyatekha Memorial Fund, n.d.).
22. "Aboriginal leaders press Prince Charles on treaty issues," *CBC News*, May 21, 2014, www.cbc.ca.
23. Douglas Sanders, "Recognition in International Law," in *The Quest for Justice: Aboriginal Peoples and Aboriginal Rights*, ed. Menno Boldt and J. Anthony Long (Toronto: University of Toronto Press, 1985), 296.
24. Ibid, 297.
25. This abbreviation means "Sensitive information that locally engaged staff overseas cannot access."
26. H.T.A. Overton, confidential letter to Sir Peter Haymen, August 1973.
27. In an earlier dispatch following the June 25–July 5 visit in 1973, Sir Peter Hayman wrote to Sir Denis Greenhill (British permanent under-secretary of state for foreign affairs and head of the diplomatic service from 1969 to 1973):

    The third important aspect was the real importance the Canadian Government attached to the visit in relation to the increasingly serious problem of the Indians and Eskimos. My friend, Jean Chrétien, the Minister of Indian and Northern Affairs, who was converted during the Queen's visit to the North in 1970 from a French Canadian Republican to a strong admirer of The Crown and of the Queen herself, has talked to me about the Crown's role in this field when I have been with him in the North on two occasions. He was sure that The Queen's visit would be significant here. And so it was.

28. Sir Peter Hayman, "The Monarchy in Canada, 1973," confidential despatch to Sir Alec Douglas-Home, August 24, 1973.
29. Honourable James K. Bartleman, "Address to gathering on grounds of Stephen Leacock Museum," (speech, Orillia, ON, September 21, 2002).
30. Ralph Steinhauer's grandfather was the Methodist missionary Henry Steinhauer (ca. 1818–1884), an Ojibwe-Anishinaabe man from the Chippewas of Rama First Nation.

31. Caen Bly, "Steinhauer Takes Oath of Office," *Edmonton Journal*, July 3, 1974, 35.
32. Alfred Thomas Neitsch, "A Tradition of Vigilance: The Role of Lieutenant Governor of Alberta," *Canadian Parliamentary Review*, Winter 2007, 23.
33. Jim Davies, *Edmonton Journal*, July 12, 1976.
34. Lois Hammond, "As Old as Alberta," *Alberta Magazine*, July/August 1980, 34.
35. Gina Blondin, "Born on the Farm, Back to the Farm," *The Native People* 12, no. 25: 2.
36. Jeff Sallott, "Discreet silence required in viceregal post," *Globe and Mail*, July 18, 1979, 9.
37. Steinhauer, The Hon. Ralph (1979, July 4), "Royal Assent Address," Alberta *Hansard*, Legislative Assembly, 19th Legislature, 1st Session.
38. Windspeaker Staff, "Prime Minister/First Nations singing from different songbooks," *Windspeaker* 22, vol 10, (1993), www.ammsa.com.
39. The Legislative Assembly of Alberta points out that Sir William McDougall was turned back from Fort Garry by Louis Riel's army before he could be officially installed as lieutenant governor, causing many historians to deny him this historical footnote. *The Legislative Assembly of Alberta*, October 3, 2014, www.assembly.ab.ca.
40. All funds for the summer reading camps were raised by the Office of the Lieutenant Governor of Ontario, and continue to be held in trust by Frontier College which now runs the camps on behalf of the vice-regal office.
41. Office of the Premier of British Columbia, *Press Release: HAND-CARVED CANOE A GIFT FOR BRITISH COLUMBIANS*, April 21, 2010.
42. Honourable Steven L. Point, lieutenant governor of British Columbia, "Address during the raising of Hosaqami," September 8, 2012.
43. Part of the grassroots "Idle No More" movement that began in 2012.
44. Honorable Grayden Nicholas, *CBC News*, January 16, 2013.
45. His Excellency David Johnston, governor general of Canada, "Opening remarks," Crown/First Nations Gathering, January 24, 2012.
46. Jennifer Ashawasegai, "Prime Minister/ First Nations singing from different songbooks," *Windspeaker* 2, vol. 29, (2012), www.ammsa.com.
47. Dean Neu and Richard Therrien, *Accounting for Genocide: Canada's Bureaucratic Assault on Aboriginal People* (Winnipeg: Fernwood Publishing, 2003), 30.
48. *The Union of Nova Scotia Indians*, last modified April 2, 2014, www.unsi.ns.ca/treaty-day.

# NOTES

49. Honourable Vaughn Solomon Schofield, lieutenant governor of Saskatchewan, *Remarks at the* "Treaty 6 and Métis Flag Raising at Saskatoon City Hall," October 25, 2013.
50. Government of Saskatchewan, "Saskatchewan's Aboriginal Peoples," last modified October 19, 2014, www.gov.sk.ca.
51. Honourable Vaughn Solomon Schofield, lieutenant governor of Saskatchewan, 2014 NAIG Opening Ceremonies, July 20, 2014.
52. Carol Goar, "Ontario's Lieutenant Governor David Onley leaves his mark," *Toronto Star*, January 9, 2014, sec. A.
53. *End of Mandate Report: The Hon. David C. Onley (2007–2014)* (Toronto: Office of the Lieutenant Governor of Ontario, 2014), 12.
54. It was the English that referred to these men using the European designation of "King." In fact, the men were representatives of the Mohawk and Mahican peoples.
55. *The Four Kings of Canada* (London: John Baker, 1710), 13.
56. Ibid, 14.
57. The Royal Household defines a Royal Chapel as follows: "The term Chapel Royal did not originally refer to a building but an establishment. It is a body of priests and singers to serve the spiritual needs of the Sovereign. Over time the term has become associated with a number of chapels used by monarchs for worship over the centuries." The British Monarchy, last modified March 6, 2014, www.royal.gov.uk.
58. Her Majesty's Chapel of the Mohawks (elevated by King Edward VII in 1904) in Six Nations of the Grand River and Her Majesty's Chapel Royal of the Mohawks (elevated by Queen Elizabeth II in 2004) in Tyendinaga.
59. Jason Millar, "Natives thrilled by surprise gift from Queen," *The Intelligencer*, July 6, 2010, www.intelligencer.ca.
60. Linda Powless, "Editorial: Queen visit should have been Memorable," *Turtle Island News*, July 7, 2010.
61. Colin G. Calloway, *Pen and Ink Witchcraft: Treaties and Treaty Making in American Indian History* (Toronto: Oxford University Press, 2013), 10.
62. "First Nation leaders seek meeting with Queen," *CBC News*, May 22, 2012, www.cbc.ca.
63. "Significance of Treaties Reaffirmed Through Historic Royal Visit," *Saskatchewan Indian* 3, no. 30 (2001), www.sicc.sk.ca/archive/saskindian/a01fal03.htm.

64. David Lilley, "Prince Charles gets a new Aboriginal name," *Saskatchewan Sage*, 9, vol. 5, (2001), www.ammsa.com.
65. "Significance of Treaties Reaffirmed Through Historic Royal Visit," *Saskatchewan Indian* 30. no. 3 (Fall 2001): 3.
66. "Aboriginal Initiatives," *Prince's Charities Canada*, www.princescharities.ca, December 7, 2014.
67. *Province of Nova Scotia*, Public Registrar of Arms, Supporters and Flags, July 20, 2007, vol. V, 160.

### Chapter Four: Building Community — A Model Royal Visit

1. Deborah Steel, "Ditidaht receives British Royals to open new library," *Ha-Shilth-Sa,*, www.hashilthsa.com. September 16, 2014.
2. Ruth Ann Onley, "How We Build a New Relationship with Ontario's First Nations," *Globe and Mail*, September 22, 2014, www.globeandmail.com.
3. Email to author, August 13, 2014.
4. Countess of Wessex, "Address to Nipissing University," (speech, Nipissing University, September 19, 2014).
5. Ruth Ann Onley, "How we build a new relationship with Ontario's First Nations"
6. Countess of Wessex, "Address to Nipissing University," (speech, Nipissing University, September 19, 2014).
7. Douglas Saunders, "Recognition in International Law," in *The Quest for Justice: Aboriginal Peoples and Aboriginal Rights*, ed. Menno Boldt and J. Anthony Long (Toronto: University of Toronto Press, 1985), 302–03.
8. Ruth Ann Onley, "How we build a new relationship with Ontario's First Nations."

### Chapter Five: Suggestions for Moving Forward Together

1. Honourable Steven L. Point, telephone conversation with author, August 28, 2014.
2. James Hammond, email message to author, November 14, 2014.
3. Queen Elizabeth II is sometimes referred to as *Te kōtuku-rerenga-tahi*, meaning "the white heron of a single flight," in Māori.

## NOTES

4. Gavin McLean, *The Governors: New Zealand's Governors and Governors Generals* (Dunedin, NZ: Otago University Press, 2006), 316–50.
5. Alan Corbiere, "The Treaty of Niagara: Living Treaty and the Necessity of Corporate Memory" (lecture, University of Toronto, August 1, 2014).
6. In am indebted to Dr. David Smith for this line of thought. It was during a conversation with Dr. Smith that the discontinuity of the Canadian Crown as an institution was raised. April 18, 2014.
7. The precise definition must be created in consultation with First Nations.
8. Office of the Lieutenant Governor of British Columbia, *Splendor in Unity: 2013 Annual Statement of the Lieutenant Governor of British Columbia* (Victoria: Government of British Columbia, 2013), 4.
9. Honourable Steven L. Point, telephone conversation with author, August 28, 2014.
10. Bruce Morito, *An Ethic of Mutual Respect: The Covenant Chain and Aboriginal-Crown Relations* (Vancouver: UBC Press, 2012), 27.
11. *Nation to Nation: A Resource on Treaties in Ontario* (North Bay: Union of Ontario Indians, 2013), 53.
12. Indian and Northern Affairs Canada, *Restructuring the Relationship*, vol. 2 of the *Report of the Royal Commission on Aboriginal Peoples* (Ottawa: Indian and Northern Affairs Canada, 2006), 244 n. 14.
13. Honourable David Zimmer, minister of aboriginal affairs (Ontario), "Address to the 24 Nations Assembled at Niagara," (speech, Niagara-on-the-Lake, August 2, 2014).
14. Peter Russell, "Tsilhqot'in Nation v. British Columbia: Can the Successful Defence of Aboriginal Title in Courts Pave the Way to Reconciliation?" (lecture, University of Toronto, 2014).
15. D. Michael Jackson, *The Crown and Canadian Federalism* (Toronto: Dundurn Press, 2013), 243.
16. The Queen v. The Secretary of State for Foreign and Commonwealth Affairs [1981] 4 C.N.L.R., quoted in Jackson, *The Crown and Canadian Federalism*, 243.
17. Greg Poelzer and Ken Coates, "Aboriginal Peoples and the Crown in Canada: Completing the Canadian Experiement," in *Continuity and Change in Canadian Politics: Essays in Honour of David E. Smith*, ed. Hans J. Michelmann and Cristine de Clercy (Toronto: University of Toronto Press, 2006), 149.

18. *About Us*, BC Treaty Commission, www.bctreaty.net, November 20, 2014.
19. Philippe Lagassé, "Canada's Citizenship Oath and the Symbolic Canadian Crown?" Thoughts on the Crown in Canada, http://lagassep.wordpress.com.

# Bibliography

Asch, Michael, ed. *Aboriginal and Treaty Rights in Canada*. Vancouver: University of British Columbia Press, 1997.

Aspinall, A. *The Later Correspondance of George III*. Vol. 1. Cambridge: Cambridge University Press, 1962.

Bagehot, Walter. *The English Constitution*. London: Little, Brown, 1873.

Beardy, Regional Chief Stan. "Urgent Open Letter to Her Majesty The Queen." December 20, 2012.

Boldt, Menno, and J. Anthony Long, eds. *The Quest for Justice: Aboriginal Peoples and Aboriginal Rights*. Toronto: University of Toronto Press, 1985.

Borrows, John. "Constitutional Principles Regulating Interaction between First Nations and the Crown." Ph.D. diss., University of Toronto, 1994.

———. "Fragile Freedoms: Indigenous Love, Law and Land in Canada's Constitution." *Ideas with Paul Kennedy*, CBC. March 5, 2014.

———. "Wampum at Niagara: The Royal Proclamation, Canadian Legal History, and Self Government." In *Aboriginal and Treaty Rights in Canada*, edited by Michael Asch. Vancouver: University of British Columbia Press, 1997.

Boyce, Peter. *The Queen's Other Realms: The Crown and Its Legacy in Australia, Canada and New Zealand*. Sydney, AU: Federation Press, 2008.

Calloway, Colin G. *Pen and Ink Witchcraft: Treaties and Treaty Making in American Indian History*. Toronto: Oxford University Press, 2013.

———, ed. *The World Turned Upside Down: Indian Voices from Early America*. New York: Bedford/St. Martin's, 1994.

Canada. *Final Report of the Royal Commission on Aboriginal Peoples*. Ottawa: Royal Commission on Aboriginal Peoples, 1996.

Canadian Charter of Rights and Freedoms, s 2, Part I of the Constitution Act, 1982, being Schedule B to the Canada Act 1982 (UK), 1982, c 11.

Carstens, Peter. *The Queen's People: A Study of Hegemony, Coercion, and Accommodation among the Okanagan of Canada*. Toronto: University of Toronto Press, 1991.

Corbiere, Alan Ojiig. "Gchi-Miigisaabiigan: The Great Wampum Belt."

*Anishinabek News*, September 2006.

——. *"Their own forms of which they take most notice": Diplomatic metaphors and symbolism on Wampum belts.* Anishinaabewin Niiwin: Four Rising Winds, 2013.

Dowd, Gregory Evans. *War Under Heaven.* Baltimore: Johns Hopkins University Press, 2002.

*End of Mandate Report: The Hon. David C. Onley (2007–2014).* Toronto: Office of the Lieutenant Governor of Ontario, 2014.

Flexner, James Thomas. *Mohawk Baronet: A Biography of Sir William Johnson.* Syracuse, NY: Syracuse University Press, 1989.

Flick, C., ed. *The Papers of Sir William Johnson.* Vol. IV. Albany, NY: University of the State of New York, 1925.

*The Four Kings of Canada.* London: John Baker, 1710.

Goar, Carol. "Ontario's Lieutenant Governor David Onley leaves his mark." *Toronto Star*, January 9 2014, sec. A.

Hamilton, Milton W. *The Papers of Sir William Johnson.* Vol. XI. Albany, NY: University of the State of New York, 1953.

Henderson, Jennifer, and Pauline Wakeham, eds. *Reconciling Canada: Critical Perspectives of the Culture of Redress.* Toronto: University of Toronto Press, 2013.

Jackson, D. Michael. *The Crown and Canadian Federalism.* Toronto: Dundurn Press, 2013.

Jackson, D. Michael, and Philippe Lagassé, eds. *Canada and the Crown: Essays on Constitutional Monarchy.* Montreal & Kingston: McGill-Queen's University Press, 2013.

Jones, Peter. *Life and journals of Keh-ke-wa-guo-na-ba: (Rev. Peter Jones,): Wesleyan Missionary.* Toronto: Anson Green, 1860.

King, Thomas. *The Truth About Stories.* Toronto: Anansi, 2003.

*Legacy of Hope and Healing.* Ottawa: Legacy of Hope Foundation, 2011.

MacKinnon, Frank. *The Crown in Canada.* Calgary: Glenbow-Alberta Institute, 1976.

McLean, Gavin. *The Governors: New Zealand's Governors and Governors General.* Dunedin, NZ: Otago University, 2006.

Michelmann, Hans J., and Cristine de Clercy, eds. *Continuity and Change in Canadian Politics: Essays in Honour of David E. Smith.* Toronto: University of Toronto Press, 2006.

# BIBLIOGRAPHY

Miller, James. *Compact, Contract, Covenant: Aboriginal Treaty-Making in Canada*. Toronto: University of Toronto Press, 2009.

Monet, Jacques. *The Canadian Crown*. Toronto: Irwin & Company, 1979.

Morito, Bruce. *An Ethic of Mutual Respect: The Covenant Chain and Aboriginal-Crown Relations*. Vancouver: UBC Press, 2012.

Morris, Alexander. *The Treaties of Canada with the Indians of Manitoba and the North-West Territories*. Toronto: Coles Publishing, 1971.

*Nation to Nation: A Resource on Treaties in Ontario*. North Bay, ON: Union of Ontario Indians, 2013.

Neitsch, Alfred Thomas. "A Tradition of Vigilance: The Role of the Lieutenant Governor of Alberta." *Canadian Parliamentary Review* 30, no. 4 (2007).

Neu, Dean, and Richard Therrien. *Accounting for Genocide: Canada's Bureaucratic Assault on Aboriginal People*. Winnipeg: Fernwood Publishing, 2003.

Office of the Lieutenant Governor of British Columbia. *Splendor in Unity: 2013 Annual Statement of the Lieutenant Governor of British Columbia*. Victoria: Government of British Columbia, 2013.

O'Toole, Fintan. *White Savage*. New York: Farrar, Straus and Giroux, 2005.

Radforth, Ian. *Royal Spectacle: The 1860 Visit of the Prince of Wales to Canada and the United States*. Toronto: University of Toronto Press, 2004.

Richter, Daniel K. "Indian-Colonist Conflicts and Alliances." In *Encyclopedia of the North American Colonies*, edited by Jacob Ernest Cooke, 223–36. New York: Charles Scribner's Sons, 1993.

Richter, Daniel K., and James H. Merrell. *Beyond the Covenant Chain: The Iroquois and Their Neighbours in Indian North America, 1600–1800*. Syracuse, NY: Syracuse University Press, 1987.

Russell, Peter. *Understanding Canada: A Country Based on Incomplete Conquests*. Toronto: University of Toronto Press, 2014.

Smith, David B. *Mississauga Portraits: Ojibwe Voices from Nineteenth-Century Canada*. Toronto: University of Toronto Press, 2013.

Smith, David E. *The Invisible Crown: The First Principle of Canadian Government*. Toronto: University of Toronto Press, 1995 (reprinted with a new preface by the author, 2013).

Smith, Jennifer, and D. Michael Jackson, eds. *The Evolving Canadian Crown*. Montreal & Kingston: McGill-Queen's University Press, 2012.

Spence, Chief Theresa. "An open letter to National Chief of the Assembly of First Nations, Nishnewbe Aski Nation Grand Chief and Ontario Regional Chief, Chiefs of Ontario." January 7, 2014.

Sullivan, James, ed. *The Papers of William Johnson.* Vol. III. Albany, NY: New York University State Press, 1962.

Tehanetorens. *Wampum Belts of the Iroquois.* Summertown, TN: Book Publishing Company, 1999.

Tidridge, Nathan. "Waterdown Natural Area Report to the City of Hamilton." May 30, 2014.

## Websites

Assembly of First Nations (www.afn.ca)
BC Treaty Commission (www.bctreaty.net)
Chiefs of Ontario (www.chiefs-of-ontario.ca)
Christ Church – Her Majesty's Chapel Royal of the Mohawk (www.chapelroyal.ca)
Frontier College (www.frontiercollege.ca)
Island of Great Spirit: The Legacy of Manitoulin (www.visualheritage.caw/manitoulin) Her Majesty's Royal Chapel of the Mohawks (www.mohawkchapel.ca)
Office of the Governor General of Canada (www.gg.ca)
Office of the Lieutenant Governor of Alberta (www.lieutenantgovernor.ab.ca)
Office of the Lieutenant Governor of British Columbia (www.ltgov.bc.ca)
Office of the Lieutenant Governor of Manitoba (www.manitobalg.ca)
Office of the Lieutenant Governor of New Brunswick (www.gnb.ca/lg)
Office of the Lieutenant Governor of Newfoundland and Labrador (www.govhouse.nl.ca)
Office of the Lieutenant Governor of Nova Scotia (www.lt.gov.ns.ca)
Office of the Lieutenant Governor of Ontario (www.lgontario.ca)
Office of the Lieutenant Governor of Prince Edward Island (www.gov.pe.ca/lg)
Office of the Lieutenant Governor of Quebec (www.lieutenant-gouverneur.qc.ca)
Office of the Lieutenant Governor of Saskatchewan (www.ltgov.sk.ca)
Official Website of the Canadian Crown (www.canadiancrown.gc.ca)
Prince's Charities Canada (www.princescharities.ca)
SayITFirst (www.sayitfirst.ca)
Six Nations Legacy Consortium (www.sixnationslegacy.org)

# BIBLIOGRAPHY

Six Nations Polytechnic (www.snpolytechnic.com)
Souharissen Natural Area (www.tidridge.com/souharissen-natural-area-waterdown.html)
The Treaty Relations Commission of Manitoba (www.trcm.ca)
Treaty Seven Management Corporation (www.treaty7.org)
Truth and Reconciliation Commission of Canada (www.trc.ca)
Woodland Cultural Centre (www.woodland-centre.on.ca)

# Index

2924 (Khowutzun) Army Cadet Corps, 99

Aberdeen, Earl of (John Hamilton-Gordon), 88
Acland, Sir Henry, 88, *89*
Ahousaht First Nation, 114
Ahtahkakoop, Chief, 103
Alberta Human Rights and Civil Liberties Association, 94
Alexis, Tyler, 12
Algonquin Nation, 57
Amherst, Lord Jeffery, 53–55
Anderson, Professor Judy, 114, *115*
Anishinaabe, 12, 19, 30, 34, 35, 36, 53, 54, *58*, 59, 67, 83, 84, 85, 93, 101, 109, *110*, 124
Anne, Princess Royal, *90*, 109, 116
Anne, Queen, 109–10
   Queen Anne Silver, 110
Archibald, Honourable Adams, *40*, 41
Articles of Capitulation (Montreal), 53
Assembly of First Nations, 80, 101, 107, 109
   National Treaty Forum (2013), 81
Association of Iroquois and Allied Indians, 16
Atleo, National Chief Shawn A-in-chut, 81, 91, 107, *108*

*Baaga'adowe*, 54
Bagehot, Walter, 17, 18, 81, 151
Balmoral Castle, Scotland, 70, *72*
Barnhart, the Honourable Gordon, 104, 116
Bartleman, Honourable James K., 92, 96, 98, 99, 106, 124
Beardy, Ontario Regional Chief Stan, 80, *90*, 98, 125
Beaver Wars. *See* Seven Years War
Bellegarde, Chief Perry, 112, *113*

Beothuk supporters, 116
Bernard, Chief Darlene, 105
*Beyond Mainland*, 30
Bill C-33 (First Nations Control of First Nations Education Act), 88
Blackfoot Confederacy, 112
Bolger, Right Honourable Jim, 134
Borrows, Dr. John, 32, 34, 53, 71
Bradstreet, Colonel John, 69
Brant, Molly, 61
British Columbia Treaty Commission, 149
British Crown. *See* Crown
Burnham, Rocky, *27*

Caledonia Land Claim, 31
Campbell, Honourable Gordon, 71
Campbell, Chief Ian, 107
Canada
   "First Confederation," 71
   Province of, 86
Canada Act (1982), 78
Canadian Bill of Rights, 74
Canadian Charter of Rights and Freedoms, 74, 153
"Canadian coat of arms." *See* Queen's Arms in Right of Canada
Canadian Constitution. *See* Constitution
Canadian Crown. *See* Crown
Canadian government
   Department of Indian and Northern Affairs, 75–76
   Ministry of Aboriginal Affairs and Northern Development, 73
Canadian Heraldic Authority, 117
Canadian Oath to the Queen, 152
Canadian Rangers, 115, *120*
Carnegie, Tania, 120–21

Carstens, Peter, 41, 75, 76,
Carter, Sarah, 36, 37
Catherine, Duchess of Cambridge, 109, 115–16
Cayuga Nation, 57, *61*, *144*
Charles II, 136
Charles, Prince of Wales, 70, 88, 90, 109, 111–15, 140, *150*
Charlottetown Accord, 97
Charlottetown Conference, 47
Chiefs of Ontario, 16
Chippewa Nation, 57
Chippewas of Mnjikaning (Rama) First Nation, 92, *98*
Chrétien, Right Honourable Jean, 92, 96
Christ Church, Her Majesty's Royal Chapel of the Mohawks, Tyendinaga Mohawk Territory, *110*, *111*
Clarkson, Right Honourable Adrienne, 37
Coates, Dr. Ken, 146, 148
Confederation, 47, 73, 75, 78, 126, 131, 148, 153–54
Congress of Aboriginal Peoples (CAP) (formerly Native Council of Canada), 97
Constitution (of Canada), 44, 79, 94, 131, 147, 150, 151
  British, 153
  Canada's, 32, 74
  Canadian, 13, 15, 38, 91, 126
Constitutional monarchy, 15, 17, 18, 77, 79, 86, 96, 117, 126, 129, 135, 137, 141, 146, 147, 148, 150, 151
Corbiere, Alan Ojiig, 52, 53, 61, 65–67, 135
Cornwallis, Lieutenant General Edward, 101–02
Council of the Mississaugas of the New Credit First Nation, 23
Council of Niagara (1764), 16, 53, *59*, 75, 112, *143*, 153. *See also* Treaty of Niagara
Council of Treaty One, 41
Courchene, David, 90
Covenant Chain of Friendship (Covenant Chain), 11, 12, 19, 23, 24, 38, 39, 41, 49, 50, 52, 56, 60–68, 74, 75, 80, 81, 85–87, 91, 93, 101, 105, 106, 111, 118, 131, 135, 137, 141, 148, 154
Covenant Chain Wampum 1764, 19–21, 52, 60–63, 66, 67, 68, 81, 82, 101, 112, 144
  Replica, 20–22, 24, 45, 52, 62, 64, 101, 112, 143, 144
Crown, 11, 19, 31, 32, 37, 39
  British Crown, 12, 15, 21, 49, 53, 54, 56, 66, 70, 82, 88, 134, 146–49
  Canadian Crown, 12, 14, 15, 17, 19, 31, 32, 77–82, 87, 91, 103, 105–09, 117, 122, 124, 126–43, 146–54
  Corporate memory, 131–36,
  Crown/First Nations relationship, 35, 38
  Dignified Crown/Dignified Canadian Crown, 17–19, 32, 36, 38, 47, 75, 77–81, 86, 92, 93, 96, 100, 102, 104, 109, 112, 117, 118, 122, 124, 126, 129, 130, 131, 134, 135, 137, 139–41, 144–54
  Efficient Crown, 38, 77, 100, 129, 141, 151–53
  French Crown, 12, 47, 49, 53
  Indigenous recognition needed, 146–50
  New Zealand (Kiwi) Crown, 133–34
Cree Nation, 37, 57, 93, 96, 104, 113, 116. *See also* Nēhiraw Nation

Danyluk, Stephanie, 32
Day, Chief Isadore, 101
de Launay, David, *142*
de Rigaud, Pierre, Marquis de Vaudreuil, 53
Dene Nation, 115
Deyohahá:ge: Indigenous Knowledge Centre (Oshweken, Ontario), 59
Dignified Crown. See Crown
Ditidaht Nation, 121
Douglas Treaties, 149
Dowd, Professor Evans, 36, 47, 54
Dowdeswell, Honourable Elizabeth, 106, 119, *120*, 124, *127*
Doxtater, Michael, 46
Dumont, Honourable W. Yvon, 96–97
Dutch (settlers and traders), 12, 63, *64*, 67–68

# INDEX

Edgar, Elder Fran, 121
Edgar, Lucy, 121
Edward Augustus, Prince (Duke of Kent), 82
Edward, Prince (Earl of Wessex), 116, 121
Edward, Prince of Wales, 83, *87*, 88
    as King Edward VII, 88
Edward, Prince of Wales (future King Edward VIII), 112
Efficient Crown. *See* Crown
Eldon, Dan, 26
Elizabeth II, Queen of Canada, 18, 35, 37, 38, 40–41, 77, 80, 91, 100, 104, 105, 109–11, 122, 126, 134 *145*, 147, 148, 151–53
Elizabeth II, Queen of New Zealand, 134
Elizabeth II, Queen of the United Kingdom of Great Britain and Northern Ireland, 146–48
Everest, Cindy, 22

Familial relationships (Crown and Indigenous Peoples), 21, 37, 41, 42, 46, 65, 80, 85, 136
Federation of Saskatchewan Indian Nations, 112
First Nations University of Canada, 70–72, 114–16
Fort Detroit, 55
Fort Michilimackinac, 54, 60
Fort Niagara, 16, 19, 52, 53, 55, 57–60, *66*, 137
Fort Pitt, 55
Fox Lake (Muskoka), 29
Francis, Chief Brian, 105
French and Indian Wars, 49. *See also* Seven Years War
French Crown. *See* Crown
Friendship Wampum. *See* Wampum

Gage, General Thomas), 55, 56, 69
George III, King, 31, 35, 37, 49, 53, 55, 67, 69, 71, 74, 77, 82, *111*
    Royal Proclamation (1763), 31, 49, 50–53, 55–57, 59, 71, 73–75, 80, 81, 155, 156, 158, 159, 161

Canada's Magna Carta, 31, 53, 145
Gift-giving, 54, 99, 129, 141–45, 153. *See also* Indigenous diplomacy
Glenelg, Lord (Charles Grant, 1st Baron Glenelg), 84
Gordon Residential School, *45*
Grand Keptin, 102–03
Grant, Brigadier General (Ret'd), Honourable John James, *102*
Great Council (of Niagara). *See* Council of Niagara
Great Lakes watershed, 19, 47, 54
Great Spirit, 87, 95
*Guerin v. The Queen* (1984), 71
Guichon, Honourable Judith, 107, *108*, 121
*Gustoweh* (headdress), *61*

Hagerman, Honourable Barbara, 104–05
Hammond, James, 132
Harawira, Hinewhare, 134
Harper, Grand Chief David, 111
Harper, Right Honourable Stephen, 46, 96
Harry, Prince, 116
Haudenosaunee/Haudenosaunee Confederacy, 12, 19, 56–59, 61, 63, 65, 67, 68, 87, 109, 110
Haverstock, Honourable Dr. Lynda, 104
Hayman, Sir Peter, 91, 92
Hayman, Vicki, 119
Head, Sir Francis Bond, 68
Hill, David Octavius, *83*
Hill, Rick, 59, *66*, 144
Honour of the Crown, 49, 81, 137, 140, 143, 154
*Hosaqami*, 99
Howard, Kirk, 19
Hughes, Alex, 155
Hunt, Chief Tony, 99
Huron Nation, 57

Idle No More movement, 78, 100
Indian Act (1876), 12, 13, 75, 76, 100, 129
Indian Association of Alberta, 91, 147

• 177 •

"Indian Chief's Medal," 11
Indian Council House (Niagara-on-the Lake), 16
Indian Residential School System, 33, 41, 44, 47, 75, 105, 107, 121, 130
Indigenous Bar Association, 49
    2013 Annual General Meeting, 49-53, 61, 80, 81
Indigenous diplomacy/protocol, 37-49, 54-57, 59, 60-66, 70, 71, 73-75, 131-36, 141-45, 153-54. See also Gift-giving
Institute for the Study of the Crown in Canada (Massey College), 32
Inuit, 12, 13, 138
Ipperwash Crisis, 31

Jackson, Dr. D. Michael, 146, 147
Jacobs, Jamie, 63
Jean, Right Honourable Michaëlle, 104, 107, *138, 145*
Johnson, Sir William, 19, 37, 38, *50*, 54, 55, 57-61, 63, 64, 66-69, 137
Johnston, Right Honourable David, 73, 78, 79, 101, 107
Johnston, Mrs. Sharon, 106
Jones, Reverend Peter. See Kahkewaquonaby
Joyal, Honourable Serge, 15

Kahgee, Eugene (Ishkwegiizhig), 23, 75
Kahkewaquonaby (Reverend Peter Jones), *83, 84*
Kainai Nation (Blood Tribe), 37
Keewatin, Elder Margaret, 116
KI Nation. See Kitchenuhmaykoosib Inninuwug, 122
King, Dr. Bernice, *108*
King, Carolyn, 23
King, Dr. Hayden, 68, 71
King, Thomas, 45, 46
King's Fire, 16, 142-43
Kitchenuhmaykoosib Inninuwug, Ontario (KI), 19, 119-28
Kiwi Crown. See New Zealand Crown
Lacrosse. See Baaga'adowe

Lagassé, Dr. Philippe, 152
Land Title Amendment Act (Alberta, 1977), 94
Lang, Otto, 93
Language, role of, 33-47, 52, 54, 125, 132, 153
Lee, Honourable Philip S., 107
Lennox Island Mi'kmaq First Nation, 104-05
*Letters Patent Constituting the Office of Governor General and Commander in Chief of Canada*, 79
Lewis, Mrs. Dorothy, 105
Lewis, Honourable H. Frank, 105
Lewis, Stephen, 47, 48
Lieutenant Governor's Aboriginal Summer Reading Camps (Ontario), 97
Linear approach to history, 31
Lockwood, William, 87
Love, familial, 15, 34, 35
    Indigenous perspective, 32-33, 43-44, 47, 88

Macdonald, Right Honourable Sir John A., 86
MacDonald, Jaden, *102*
MacKay, Alex, *21*, 32
MacKay, Eva, 46
Madahbee, Grand Council Chief Patrick "Pat," 16, *66*, 142
Maliseet Nation, 65, 100, 116, 139
Management of Indian Lands and Property Act (Indian Land Act) (1860), 86
Manitoba Indian Brotherhood, 90
Manitoba Keewatinowi Okimakanak, 111
Manitoba Métis Federation, 97
Manitoulin Island Treaty (1836). See Treaty
Māori, 132-34
Martin, Mungo, 99
Martin, Peter. See Oronhyatekha
Maracle, Ken, 19, *20*, *21*, 24, *45*, 61, *62*, 144
Maracle, Chief R. Donald, 111
Marshall, Grand Chief Donald Sr., 103
Marshall, John (American chief justice), 14
Mateparae, Lt. Gen., Rt. Hon. Sir Jerry, 133

# INDEX

McDougall, Honourable Sir William, 97
McLeod, Captain Norman, 60
Mékaisto, Chief, 112
Membertou, Grand Chief, 105
Merritt, Richard, 60
Métis, 12, 96, 97, 103, 138
Mi'kmaq Nation, 26, 65, 84, 101–05, 139
Miller, Dr. J.R. (Jim), 32, 52, 87, 157–58
Mississaugas of the New Credit, 23, 26, *27*, 83–86, 155–56
Mistawasis, Chief, 103
Mohawk Chapel. *See* Royal Chapel of the Mohawks
Mohawk Institute Residential School (Mush Hole), 44, 75
Mohawk Nation, 57, 61, 67, 88, *110*, 111
Mohawks of the Bay of Quinte, 109
Mohican Nation, 57
Morgan, Justice Edward, 152
Morito, Dr. Bruce, 34, 35, 42, 65
Morris, Honourable Alexander, 37–*39*, 41, 103
Morris, Chief Danny, 122, *127*
Mulroney, Right Honourable Brian, 96
Mush Hole, *45*. *See also* Mohawk Institute (Residential School)

Nahnebahwequay (Catherine Sutton), 83
*Nation to Nation: A Resource on Treaties in Ontario*, 81
"Nation to Nation" relationships, 14, 112, 144, 148–49
National Aboriginal Week, 120
Nēhiraw Nation, 37, 38, 95. *See also* Cree Nation
Nekaneet First Nation, 113
Nepinak, Grand Chief Derek, 88, 90
New Great Council, 153–54
New Zealand, 132, 133
    Dignified Crown, 133
    Waitangi Day, 133–34
    Treaty of Waitangi (1840), 134
New Zealand Crown (Kiwi Crown). *See* Crown

Niagara Council (1764). *See* Council of Niagara
Nicholas, Honourable Graydon, 96, 100
Nipissing Nation, 57
Nisga'a First Nation, 149
Nishnawbe Aski Nation, 80
Nkwala, Chief, 75
North West Company, 37

Oakes, Elder Gordon, 113
Odawa Nation, 36, 54, 57, 66
Ojibwe Nation, 55, 113
Oka Crisis, 31
Onley, Honourable David C., 16, 23, *24, 66*, 81, 82, 86, 99, 105–07, 119, 120, 124
Onley, Ruth Ann, 106, 119, *120,* 122, 125, *127*
Onondaga Nation, 22, 57, 63, 67
Oral History, 42–43, 160
Oral Tradition, 31, 43, 52, 74
Oronhyatekha, Dr. (Peter Martin), 87–*89*
Overton, H.T.A., 92

Partridge, Councillor Judi, 23
Pawnee Nation, 57
Pelham-Clinton, Henry (Duke of Newcastle), 83, 86
Pennefather, Richard, 86
Petitions, 90–91, 126, 139–41, 146
Poelzer, Dr. Greg, 146, 148
Point, Gwendolyn, 107, *108*
Point, Honourable Steven L., 46, 69, 71, 78, 96, 99, 100, 107, *108,* 130, 136, 161, 164
Pontiac (Odawa Chief), 54
Pontiac's War (1763–1766), 53
Potawatomie Nation, 57

Quahog beads, 52
Queen Anne Silver. *See* Anne, Queen
Queen Anne's War (1702–1713), 109
Queen's Arms
    in Right of Canada, 116
    in Right of Manitoba, 116
    in Right of New Brunswick, 116

in Right of Newfoundland and Labrador, 117
in Right of Nova Scotia, 117
in Right of Saskatchewan, 116–17
Queen's Fire, 137–39

Rama First Nation, 49, 52, 61, 98
Red River Rebellion, 97
Red River Settlement, 37
Reeves, Right Reverend and Honourable Sir Alfred Paul, 133
Responsible government, 77–81, 85, 86, 91, 94, 118, 131, 137, 139, 140, 151, 153
Robertson, Gregor, *108*
Robinson-Huron Treaty (1850), 140
Royal Canadian Navy, 99
Royal Chapel
 of the Mohawks (Six Nations), 110, 111
 of the Mohawks (Tyendinaga), 110, 111
Royal Commission on Aboriginal Peoples (1996), 42, 146
Royal Proclamation (1763). See George III, King
Russell, Dr. Peter, 14–15, 71, 77, 146

Sacred Fire, 23, *27*
Saddle Lake Cree Nation, 93, 96
Salish Nation, 37
Sallott, Jeff, 94
Sanders, Douglas, 126
Sark, John J. 105
Saugeen First Nation #29, 23
Sauk Nation, 55
Sault, Elder Garry, 23, *27*, 86
Saulteaux Nation, 37
Schofield, Honourable Vaughn Solomon, 103, 104, 165
Scott, Duncan Campbell, 45
Scott, Susan, 29
Segal, Honourable Hugh, 15
Selkirk Treaty (1817), 37
Seneca Nation, 54, 57, 63
Serpent River First Nation, 101

Seven Years War (Beaver Wars/French and Indian Wars) (1754–1763), 47, 49
Shawnee Nation, 47
Silver Covenant Chain of Friendship, 19, 23, 74
Simcoe, Honourable John Graves, 93
Sinclair, Dr. Niigaanwewidam James, 90
Sinclair, Justice Murray, 33, 47, 52, 53, 80, 81
Sioui, Grand Chief Konrad, 109
Six Nations Legacy Consortium, 16, 144
Six Nations of the Grand River, 19, *20*, *27*, 45, *62*, 63, 87, 89, 109–11
Smith, Dr. David E., 17, 18, 146
Sophie, Countess of Wessex, 18, 19, 106, 108, 116, 119–28, 139
Souharissen Natural Area (Waterdown), 23–26
Sovereignty, 13, 14, 50, 53, 55, 60, 69, 77, 130, 136, 141, 146, 148, 149
Spence, Chief Theresa, 78–80, 124, 138
Squamish First Nation, 107
St. Anne's Church (Lennox Island Mi'kmaq First Nation), 104
 St. Anne's Sunday, 104, 105
Statute of Westminster (1931), 77, 147–48
Steinhauer, Honourable Ralph Garvin, 93–96, 163–64
Stó:lō Nation, 99
Stoney Knoll First Nation, 113
Supreme Court of Canada, 14, 71
Sutton, Catherine, 83. See also Nahnebahwequay
Sweet, David (MP), 23

*Teioháte Kaswenta* (Two-Row Wampum), 46, 67, *68*, 81, 144
The Commons (Niagara-on-the-Lake), 16, 60, 142
*The English Constitution*, 17, 81
"The Reception By The Pond" (Waterdown), 24
Thomas, Yvonne, 21
Time, concept of, 31, 42–44, 61, *62*, 135

# INDEX

Tizard, Right Honourable Dame Catherine, 134
Treaty (First Nations/Crown):
    Manitoulin Island Treaty (1836), 68
    Selkirk Treaty, 37
    Treaty Eight, 146
    Treaty Five, 39
    Treaty Four, 39, 104, 116
    Treaty of Niagara, 11, 16, 21–24, 38, 39, 49-76, 86, 101, 110, 131, 142, 143, 154
    Treaty Nine, 122, 127
    Treaty of Waitangi (1840), 133–34
    Treaty One, 41
    Treaty Seven, 112, 140
    Treaty Six, 39, 103, 113, 116
    Treaty Three, 39
Treaty relationships, 42–44, 47, 56, 57, 70–76, 78, 79, 82, 85, 92, 104, 126, 130–32, 135–39, 146–49
*Treaty Canoe, 21*, 32
Treaty Day
    Nova Scotia, 102–03
    Prince Albert Urban, 116
    Prince Edward Island (defacto), 105
Trudeau, Right Honourable Pierre Elliott, 94, 96, 147
Truth and Reconciliation Commission of Canada, 16, 32, 46, 48, 81, 107, 120, *145*
Tsilhqot'in Nation, 14, 146,
Twenty-Four Nations Wampum. *See* Wampum
Two-Row Wampum. *See* Wampum
Tyendinaga Mohawk Territory, 110, 111

Union of New Brunswick Indians, 147
Union of Nova Scotia Indians, 147

Vanderwal, Christine, 19–*20*
Victoria, Queen, *11*, 35, 37, 38, 40–41, 70–*72*, 77, 82–88, 93, 105, 109, 113, 133, 153

Wabanaki Confederacy, 12
Waikato-Tainui Settlement (New Zealand), 134
Waitangi Day (New Zealand), 133–34
Wampum, 16, 19, 21, 52, 53, 56, 57, 59, 60, 61, 66, *68*, 73, 74, 75, 85, 86, 101, 109, 116, 138, 143, 144, 153
    Friendship Wampum, 64, 69, 116, 143–44
    Twenty-Four Nations Wampum, 66, 68
    Two-Row Wampum, 46, 68. *See also Teioháte Kaswenta*
Wanuskewin Heritage Park (Saskatoon), 112–13
War of 1812 (1812–1815), 15, 75, 125
Waterdown, Ontario, 22–24, 26,
Waterdown District High School, 21–22
Waterdown South Development, 22–23
Weenie, Elder Ben, 113
Weiler, Justice Karen M., 152
Wendake Nation, 109
Wesley, Elder Andrew, 106
Whitecap Dakota First Nation, 15, 32, 125
William IV, King, 68, 84
William, Duke of Cambridge, 115
Written history/documents, 42, 43, 55, 56, 59, 74
Wynne, Honourable Kathleen, 86, 106, 119, 120, 122, 125, 142

Zimmer, Honourable David, 16, 125, 142–44

# About the Author

Nathan Tidridge teaches Canadian history, government, and genocide studies at Waterdown District High School and was awarded the Premier's Award for Teaching Excellence (Teacher of the Year) in 2008. In 2011 he received the Charles Baillie Award for Excellence in Secondary School Teaching from Queen's University. In 2014 Mr. Tidridge was given the Sharon Enkin Award for Excellence in Holocaust Education by the Hamilton Jewish Federation. For the fiftieth anniversary of the proclamation of Canada's National Flag on February 15, 2015, Prime Minister Stephen Harper presented Mr. Tidridge with one of fifty specially created flags in recognition of his "tremendous contributions to our great country."

On May 22, 2012, Nathan Tidridge was one of six Ontarians presented with a Diamond Jubilee Medal by His Royal Highness The Prince of Wales for exemplifying Her Majesty's twenty-first birthday pledge: "I declare before you all that my whole life whether it be long or short shall be devoted to your service." The ceremony took place at Queen's Park in the presence of the Duchess of Cornwall, the lieutenant governor of Ontario, and Mrs. Ruth Ann Onley.

Nathan lives in Waterdown, Ontario, with his wife, Christine

## ABOUT THE AUTHOR

Vanderwal, and daughters Sophie and Elyse. His previous publications include *Prince Edward, Duke of Kent: Father of the Canadian Crown* (2013), *Canada's Constitutional Monarchy* (2011), *Beyond Mainland* (2009), and *When Summer Suns Were Glowing* (2003). He maintains a website dedicated to educating Canadians about their constitutional monarchy at www.canadiancrown.com.

**Other titles by Nathan Tidridge**

*When Summer Suns Were Glowing*

*Beyond Mainland: Exploring History and Identity in Cottage Country*

*Canada's Constitutional Monarchy: An Introduction to Our Form of Government*

*Prince Edward, Duke of Kent: Father of the Canadian Crown*